# Contents

# Easy Gluten-Free, Dairy-Free Bread

**PREP: 15 MINUTES /MAKES 12**

## Ingredients

- 1 1/2 cups warm water
- 2 teaspoons active dry yeast
- 2 teaspoons sugar
- 2 eggs, room temperature
- 1 egg white, room temperature
- 1 1/2 tablespoons apple cider vinegar
- 4 1/2 tablespoons olive oil
- 3 1/3 cups multi-purpose gluten-free flour

## Directions

### 1. Preparing the Ingredients

Add the yeast and sugar to the warm water and stir to mix in a large mixing bowl; set aside until foamy, about 8 to 10 minutes.

Whisk the 2 eggs and 1 egg white together in a separate mixing bowl and add to baking pan of bread maker.

Add apple cider vinegar and oil to baking pan.

Add foamy yeast/water mixture to baking pan.

Add the multi-purpose gluten-free flour on top.

### 2. Select the Bake cycle

Set for Gluten-Free bread setting and Start.

Remove and invert pan onto a cooling rack to remove the bread from the baking pan. Allow to cool completely before slicing to serve.

# Wheat Bran Bread

**PREP: 10 MINUTES /MAKES 1 LOAF**

## Ingredients

- 16 slice bread (2 pounds)
- 1½ cups lukewarm milk
- 3 tablespoons unsalted butter, melted
- 2 teaspoons table salt
- ½ cup wheat bran
- 3½ cups white bread flour
- 1½ cups whole-wheat bread flour
- 1 cup oat bran
- 3 cups whole-wheat bread flour
- 2 teaspoons bread machine yeast

## Directions

### 1. Preparing the Ingredients.

Measure and add the ingredients to the pan in the order mentioned above. Place the pan in the bread machine and close the lid. Place the pan in the bread machine and close the lid.

### 2. Select the Bake cycle

Turn on the bread maker. Select the White / Basic or Whole Wheat setting, then select the dough size and crust color. Press start to start the cycle.

When this is done, and the bread is baked, remove the pan from the machine. Let stand a few minutes. Remove the bread from the pan and leave it on a wire rack to cool for at least 10 minutes. Slice and serve.

# Soft Egg Bread

**PREP: 10 MINUTES /MAKES 1 LOAF**

**Ingredients**
- 16 slice bread (2 pounds)
- 1 cup milk, at 80°F to 90°F
- 5 tablespoons melted butter, cooled
- 3 eggs, at room temperature
- ⅓ cup sugar
- 2 teaspoons salt
- 4 cups white bread flour
- 1 cup oat bran
- 3 cups whole-wheat bread flour
- 1½ teaspoons bread machine or instant yeast

**Directions**
1. **Preparing the Ingredients.**
Place the ingredients in your bread machine as recommended by the manufacturer.
2. **Select the Bake cycle**
Turn on the bread maker. Select the White / Basic setting, then select the dough size and medium crust. Press Start.

When this is done, and the bread is baked, remove the pan from the machine. Let stand a few minutes. Remove the bread from the pan and leave it on a wire rack to cool for at least 10 minutes. Slice and serve.

# Date and Nut Bread

**PREP: 10 MINUTES /MAKES 1 LOAF**

**Ingredients**
- Water – 1 cup
- Oil – 1 ½ tbsp.
- Honey – 2 tbsp.
- Salt – ½ tsp.
- Rolled oats – ¾ cup
- Whole wheat flour – ¾ cup
- Bread flour – 1 ½ cups
- Active dry yeast – 1 ½ tsp.
- Dates – ½ cups, pitted and chopped
- Chopped almonds – ½ cup

**Directions**

**1. Preparing the Ingredients**

Place everything into the bread pan according to the bread machine recommendation.

**2. Select the Bake cycle**

Select Fruit bread/Basic cycle and press Start. You can add the dates and nuts after the beep or at the very beginning.

# Rye Bread

**PREP: 10 MINUTES /MAKES 1 LOAF**

**Ingredients**

- 16 slice bread (2 pounds)
- 1⅔ cups lukewarm water
- ¼ cup + 4 teaspoons Dijon mustard
- 2 tablespoons unsalted butter, melted
- 4 teaspoons sugar
- 1 teaspoon table salt
- 2 cups rye flour
- 2⅔ cups white bread flour
- 1½ teaspoons bread machine yeast

**Directions**

**1. Preparing the Ingredients.**

Measure and add the ingredients to the pan in the order mentioned above. Place the pan in the bread machine and close the lid. Place the pan in the bread machine and close the lid.

**1. Select the Bake cycle**

Turn on the bread maker. Select the White / Basic or Whole Wheat setting, then select the dough size and crust color. Press start to start the cycle.

When this is done, and the bread is baked, remove the pan from the machine. Let stand a few minutes. Remove the bread from the pan and leave it on a wire rack to cool for at least 10 minutes. Slice and serve.

# Multi-Seed Bread

**PREP: 10 MINUTES /MAKES 1 LOAF**

**Ingredients**

- Tepid water – 1 cup
- Salt – 1 tsp.
- Olive oil – 2 tbsp.
- Whole wheat bread flour – 1 cup
- White bread flour – 2 cups
- Dried yeast – 1 ½ tsp.
- Mixed seeds – 1/3 cup sesame, pumpkin, sunflower, poppy

**Directions**

**1. Preparing the Ingredients.**

Add the ingredients according to bread machine recommendation.

**2. Select the Bake cycle**

Select White bread/Basic cycle and press Start. Remove the bread when done. Cool, slice, and serve.

# Healthy Bran Bread

**PREP: 10 MINUTES /MAKES 1 LOAF**

## Ingredients

- 12 slice bread (1½ pounds)
- 1⅛ cups milk, at 80°F to 90°F
- 2¼ tablespoons melted butter, cooled
- 1½ tablespoons unsalted butter, melted
- 3 tablespoons sugar
- 1½ teaspoons salt
- ½ cup wheat bran
- 2⅔ cups white bread flour
- 1½ teaspoon bread machine or instant yeast

## Directions

**1. Preparing the Ingredients.**

Measure and add the ingredients to the pan in the order mentioned above. Place the pan in the bread machine and close the lid.

**2. Select the Bake cycle**

Turn on the bread maker. Select the White / Basic or Whole Wheat setting, then select the dough size and crust color. Press start to start the cycle.

When this is done, and the bread is baked, remove the pan from the machine. Let stand a few minutes. Remove the bread from the pan and leave it on a wire rack to cool for at least 10 minutes. Slice and serve.

# Classic Whole Wheat Bread

**PREP: 10 MINUTES /MAKES 1 LOAF**

## Ingredients

- 12 slice bread (1½ pounds)
- 1⅛ cups milk, at 80°F to 90°F
- 2¼ tablespoons melted butter, cooled
- 1½ tablespoons unsalted butter, melted
- 3 tablespoons sugar
- 1½ teaspoons salt
- ½ cup wheat bran
- ¾ cup lukewarm water
- ⅓ cup unsalted butter, melted
- 2 eggs, at room temperature
- 1½ teaspoons table salt
- 3 tablespoons sugar
- 1 cup whole-wheat flour
- 2 cups white bread flour
- 1⅔ teaspoons bread machine yeast

## Directions

**1. Preparing the Ingredients.**

Measure and add the ingredients to the pan in the order mentioned above. Place the pan in the bread machine and close the lid. Place the pan in the bread machine and close the lid.

**2. Select the Bake cycle**

Turn on the bread maker. Select the Whole Wheat setting, then select the dough size and crust color. Press start to start the cycle.

When this is done, and the bread is baked, remove the pan from the machine. Let stand a few minutes. Remove the bread from the pan and leave it on a wire rack to cool for at least 10 minutes. Slice and serve.

# Coffee Rye Bread

**PREP: 10 MINUTES /MAKES 1 LOAF**

**Ingredients**

- Lukewarm water – ½ cup
- Brewed coffee – ¼ cup, 80°F
- Dark molasses – 2 tbsp.
- Brown sugar – 5 tsp.
- Unsalted butter – 4 tsp., softened
- Powdered skim milk – 1 tbsp.
- Kosher salt – 1 tsp.
- Unsweetened cocoa powder – 4 tsp.
- Dark rye flour – 2/3 cup
- Whole-wheat bread machine flour – ½ cup
- Caraway seeds – 1 tsp.
- White bread machine flour – 1 cup
- Bread machine yeast – 1 ½ tsp

**Directions**

**1. Preparing the Ingredients**

Place everything in the bread machine pan according to the bread machine recommendation.

**2. Select the Bake cycle**

Select Basic and Light crust. Press Start. Remove the bread. Cool, slice, and serve.

# Dark Rye Bread

**PREP: 10 MINUTES /MAKES 1 LOAF**

**Ingredients**

- 12 slice bread (1½ pounds)
- 1 cup water, at 80°F to 90°F
- 1½ tablespoons melted butter, cooled
- 1½ tablespoons unsalted butter, melted
- ⅓ cup molasses
- ⅓ teaspoon salt
- 1½ tablespoons unsweetened cocoa powder
- Pinch ground nutmeg
- ¾ cup rye flour
- 2 cups white bread flour

- 1⅔ teaspoons bread machine or instant yeast

**Directions**
**1. Preparing the Ingredients.**
Place the ingredients in your bread machine as recommended by the manufacturer.
**2. Select the Bake cycle**
Turn on the bread maker. Select the White / Basic setting, then select the dough size and crust color. Press start to start the cycle.
When this is done, and the bread is baked, remove the pan from the machine. Let stand a few minutes. Remove the bread from the pan and leave it on a wire rack to cool for at least 10 minutes. Slice and serve.

# Honey Nut Bread

**PREP: 10 MINUTES /MAKES 1 LOAF**

**Ingredients**
- Eggs – 2
- Cottage cheese – 2/3 cup
- Milk – ½ cup
- Butter – ¼ cup
- Honey – 2 tbsp.
- All-purpose flour – 4 cups
- Instant yeast – 1 tbsp.
- Salt – 1 tsp.
- Candied nuts – ¾ cups, chopped

**Directions**
**1. Preparing the Ingredients**
Add everything, except nuts to your bread machine according to manufacturer recommendation.
**2. Select the Bake cycle**
Select Basic and choose Light crust type. Press Start. Add the nuts when the machine beeps. Remove the bread when ready. Cool, slice, and serve.

# Oat Bran Nutmeg Bread

**PREP: 10 MINUTES /MAKES 1 LOAF**

**Ingredients**
- 16 slice bread (2 pounds)
- 1 cup lukewarm water
- 3 tablespoons unsalted butter, melted
- ¼ cup blackstrap molasses
- ½ teaspoon table salt
- 3 cups whole-wheat bread flour
- ¼ teaspoon ground nutmeg
- 1 cup oat bran

- 3 cups whole-wheat bread flour
- 2¼ teaspoons bread machine yeast

**Directions**

**1. Preparing the Ingredients.**

Choose the size of bread to prepare. Measure and add the ingredients to the pan in the order as indicated in the ingredient listing. Place the pan in the bread machine and close the lid.

**2. Select the Bake cycle**

Turn on the bread maker. Select the White / Basic setting, then select the dough size and crust color. Press start to start the cycle. When this is done, and the bread is baked, remove the pan from the machine.

Let stand a few minutes.

Remove the bread from the pan and leave it on a wire rack to cool for at least 10 minutes. Slice and serve.

# Three-Seed Bread

**PREP: 10 MINUTES /MAKES 1 LOAF**

**Ingredients**

- Water – 2/3 cup plus 2 tsp.
- Butter – 1 tbsp., softened
- Honey – 1 tbsp.
- Sunflower seeds – 2 tbsp.
- Sesame seeds – 2 tbsp.
- Poppy seeds – 2 tbsp.
- Salt – ¾ tsp.
- Whole wheat flour – 1 cup
- Bread flour - 1 cup
- Nonfat dry milk powder – 3 tbsp.
- Active dry yeast – 2 tsp.

**Directions**

**1. Preparing the Ingredients**

Put all ingredients in the bread machine pan according to its order.

**2. Select the Bake cycle**

Select Basic bread and press Start. Remove the bread when done. Cool, slice, and serve.

# Peasant Bread

**PREP: 10 MINUTES /MAKES 12 SLICES**

**Ingredients**

- 2 tablespoons full rounded yeast
- 2 cups white bread flour
- 1 1/2 tablespoons sugar
- 1 tablespoon salt
- 7/8 cup water
- For the topping:
- Olive oil
- Poppy seeds

**Directions**

**1.  Preparing the Ingredients**

Add water first, then add the dry ingredients to the bread machine, reserving yeast.

Make a well in the center of the dry ingredients and add the yeast.

**2.  Select the Bake cycle**

Choose French cycle, light crust color, and push Start. When bread is finished, coat the top of loaf with a little olive oil and lightly sprinkle with poppy seeds. Allow to cool slightly and serve warm with extra olive oil for dipping.

# English muffin Bread

**PREP: 10 MINUTES /MAKES 1 LOAF**

**Ingredients**

- 12 slice bread (1½ pounds)
- 1¼ cups buttermilk, at 80°F to 90°F
- 1½ tablespoons melted butter, cooled
- 1½ tablespoons sugar
- 1⅛ teaspoons salt
- ⅓ teaspoon baking powder
- 2⅔ cups white bread flour
- 1⅔ teaspoons bread machine or instant yeast

**Directions**

**1.  Preparing the Ingredients.**

Place the ingredients in your bread machine as recommended by the manufacturer

**2.  Select the Bake cycle**

Close the lid, Turn on the bread maker. Select the White / Basic setting, then select the dough size, select light or medium crust. Press start to start the cycle. When this is done, and the bread is baked, remove the pan from the machine. Let stand a few minutes. Remove the bread from the skillet and leave it on a wire rack to cool for at least 10 minutes. Slice and serve.

# Golden Raisin Bread

**PREP: 10 MINUTES /MAKES 1 LOAF**

**Ingredients**

- 8 slice bread (pounds)
- ¾ cup milk, at 80°F to 90°F
- 1 tablespoon melted butter, cooled
- ¼ cup molasses
- 1 tablespoon sugar
- ¾ teaspoon salt
- 2 cups white bread flour
- 1 teaspoon bread machine or instant yeast
- ½ cup golden raisins
- 12 slice bread (1½ pounds)
- 1⅛ cups milk, at 80°F to 90°F
- 1½ tablespoons melted butter, cooled

**Directions**

1. **Preparing the Ingredients.**

Place the ingredients, except the raisins, in your bread machine as recommended by the manufacturer.

2. **Select the Bake cycle**

Program the machine for Basic/White or Sweet bread, select light or medium crust, and press Start. Add the raisins at the raisin/nut signal. When the loaf is done, remove the bucket from the machine.

Let the loaf cool for 5 minutes. Gently shake the bucket to remove the loaf, and turn it out onto a rack to cool.

# Multigrain Honey Bread

**PREP: 10 MINUTES /MAKES 1 LOAF**

## Ingredients

- 12 slice bread (1½ pounds)
- 1⅛ cups lukewarm milk
- 2¼ tablespoons unsalted butter, melted
- 3 tablespoons sugar
- 1½ teaspoons table salt
- ⅓ cup wheat bran
- 1½ tablespoons honey
- 1⅛ cups multigrain flour
- 2 cups white bread flour
- 1⅛ cups lukewarm water
- 2 tablespoons unsalted butter, melted

## Directions

1. **Preparing the Ingredients**

Choose the size of bread to prepare. Measure and add the ingredients to the pan in the order as indicated in the ingredient listing. Place the pan in the bread machine and close the lid.

2. **Select the Bake cycle**

Close the lid, Turn on the bread maker. Select the White / Basic setting, then select the dough size and crust color. Press start to start the cycle.

When this is done, and the bread is baked, remove the pan from the machine. Let stand a few minutes. Remove the bread from the skillet and leave it on a wire rack to cool for at least 10 minutes.

Slice and serve.

# Golden Corn Bread

**PREP: 10 MINUTES /MAKES 1 LOAF**

## Ingredients

- 12 to 16 slices bread (1½ to 2 pounds)
- 1 cup buttermilk, at 80°F to 90°F
- ¼ cup melted butter, cooled
- 2 eggs, at room temperature
- 1⅓ cups all-purpose flour
- 1 cup cornmeal
- ¼ cup sugar
- 2¼ cups whole-wheat bread flour

- 1½ teaspoons bread machine yeast

**Directions**

**1.  Preparing the Ingredients.**

Place the buttermilk, butter, and eggs in your in your bread machine as recommended by the manufacturer.

**2.  Select the Bake cycle**

Program the machine for Quick/Rapid bread and press Start. While the wet ingredients are mixing, stir together the flour, cornmeal, sugar, baking powder, and salt in a small bowl.

After the first fast mixing is done and the machine signals, add the dry ingredients. When the loaf is done, remove the bucket from the machine. Let the loaf cool for 5 minutes. Gently shake the bucket to remove the loaf, and turn it out onto a rack to cool.

# Classic Dark Bread

**PREP: 10 MINUTES /MAKES 1 LOAF**

**Ingredients**
- 12 slice bread (1½ pounds)
- 1 cup lukewarm water
- 1½ tablespoons unsalted butter, melted
- ⅓ cup molasses
- ⅓ teaspoon table salt
- ¾ cup rye flour
- 2 cups white bread flour
- 2¼ cups whole-wheat bread flour
- 1½ tablespoons unsweetened cocoa powder
- Pinch ground nutmeg
- 1⅔ teaspoons bread machine yeast

**Directions**

**1.  Preparing the Ingredients.**

Choose the size of bread to prepare. Measure and add the ingredients to the pan in the order as indicated in the ingredient listing. Place the pan in the bread machine and close the lid.

**2.  Select the Bake cycle**

Close the lid, Turn on the bread maker. Select the White / Basic setting, then select the dough size and crust color. Press start to start the cycle.

When this is done, and the bread is baked, remove the pan from the machine. Let stand a few minutes. Remove the bread from the skillet and leave it on a wire rack to cool for at least 10 minutes. Slice and serve.

# Classic Corn Bread

**PREP: 10 MINUTES /MAKES 1 LOAF**

**Ingredients**
- 12 slice bread (1½ pounds)

* 1 cup lukewarm buttermilk
* ¼ cup unsalted butter, melted
* 2 eggs, at room temperature
* ¼ cup sugar
* 1 teaspoon table salt
* 1⅓ cups all-purpose flour
* 1 cup cornmeal
* 1 tablespoon baking powder

**Directions**

**1. Preparing the Ingredients.**

Choose the size of bread to prepare. Measure and add the ingredients to the pan in the order as indicated in the ingredient listing. Place the pan in the bread machine and close the lid.

**2. Select the Bake cycle**

Close the lid, Turn on the bread maker. Select the White / Basic setting, then select the dough size, select light or medium crust. Press start to start the cycle.

When this is done, and the bread is baked, remove the pan from the machine. Let stand a few minutes. Remove the bread from the skillet and leave it on a wire rack to cool for at least 10 minutes. Slice and serve.

# Traditional Italian Bread

**PREP: 10 MINUTES /MAKES 1 LOAF**

**Ingredients**

* 12 slice bread (1½ pounds)
* 1 cup water, at 80°F to 90°F
* 1½ tablespoons olive oil
* 1½ tablespoons sugar
* 1⅛ teaspoons salt
* 3 cups white bread flour
* 2⅔ cups white bread flour
* 1½ teaspoons bread machine or instant yeast

**Directions**

**1. Preparing the Ingredients.**

Place the ingredients in your bread machine as recommended by the manufacturer

**2. Select the Bake cycle**

Close the lid, Turn on the bread maker. Select the White / Basic setting, then select the dough size, select light or medium crust. Press start to start the cycle.

When this is done, and the bread is baked, remove the pan from the machine. Let stand a few minutes. Remove the bread from the skillet and leave it on a wire rack to cool for at least 10 minutes. Slice and serve.

# Basic Seed Bread

## Ingredients

- 12 slice bread (1½ pounds)
- 1⅛ cups lukewarm water
- 1½ tablespoons unsalted butter, melted
- 1½ tablespoons sugar
- 1⅛ teaspoons table salt
- 2½ cups white bread flour
- ¾ cup ground chia seeds
- 2 tablespoons sesame seeds
- 1½ teaspoons bread machine yeast

## Directions

**1. Preparing the Ingredients.**

Choose the size of bread to prepare. Measure and add the ingredients to the pan in the order as indicated in the ingredient listing. Place the pan in the bread machine and close the lid.

**2. Select the Bake cycle**

Close the lid, Turn on the bread maker. Select the White / Basic setting, then select the dough size, select light or medium crust. Press start to start the cycle.

When this is done, and the bread is baked, remove the pan from the machine. Let stand a few minutes. Remove the bread from the skillet and leave it on a wire rack to cool for at least 10 minutes. Slice and serve.

# Double-Chocolate Zucchini Bread

PREP: 10 MINUTES /MAKES 1 LOAF

## Ingredients

- 225 grams grated zucchini
- 125 grams All-Purpose Flour Blend
- 50 grams all-natural unsweetened cocoa powder (not Dutch-process)
- 1 teaspoon xanthan gum
- ¾ teaspoon baking soda
- ¼ teaspoon baking powder
- ¼ teaspoon salt
- ½ teaspoon ground espresso
- 135 grams chocolate chips or nondairy alternative
- 100 grams cane sugar or granulated sugar
- 2 large eggs
- ¼ cup avocado oil or canola oil
- 60 grams vanilla Greek yogurt or nondairy alternative
- 1 teaspoon vanilla extract

## Directions

**1. Preparing the Ingredients.**

Measure and add the ingredients to the pan in the order mentioned above. Place the pan in the bread machine and close the lid.

**2. Select the Bake cycle**

Turn on the bread maker. Select the White / Basic setting, then select the dough size, select light or medium crust. Press start to start the cycle.

When this is done, and the bread is baked, remove the pan from the machine. Let stand a few minutes. Remove the bread from the skillet and leave it on a wire rack to cool for at least 15 minutes. Store leftovers in an airtight container at room temperature for up to 5 days, or freeze to enjoy a slice whenever you desire. Let each slice thaw naturally

# Basic Bulgur Bread

**PREP: 10 MINUTES /MAKES 1 LOAF**

## Ingredients

- 16 slice bread (2 pounds)
- ½ cup lukewarm water
- ½ cup bulgur wheat
- 1⅓ cups lukewarm milk
- 1⅓ tablespoons unsalted butter, melted
- 1⅓ tablespoons sugar
- 1 teaspoon table salt
- 4 cups bread flour
- 3 cups whole-wheat bread flour
- 2 teaspoons bread machine yeast

## Directions

**1. Preparing the Ingredients.**

Measure and add the ingredients to the pan in the order mentioned above. Place the pan in the bread machine and close the lid.

**2. Select the Bake cycle**

Close the lid, Turn on the bread maker. Select the White / Basic setting, then select the dough size, select light or medium crust. Press start to start the cycle.

When this is done, and the bread is baked, remove the pan from the machine. Let stand a few minutes. Remove the bread from the skillet and leave it on a wire rack to cool for at least 10 minutes. Slice and serve.

# Oat Quinoa Bread

**PREP: 10 MINUTES /MAKES 1 LOAF**

## Ingredients

- 12 slice bread (1½ pounds)
- 1 cup lukewarm milk
- ⅔ cup cooked quinoa, cooled
- ¼ cup unsalted butter, melted
- 1 tablespoon sugar
- 1 teaspoon table salt
- 1½ cups white bread flour
- ¼ cup quick oats

- ¾ cup whole-wheat flour
- 1½ teaspoons bread machine yeast

**Directions**
**1. Preparing the Ingredients.**
Measure and add the ingredients to the pan in the order mentioned above. Place the pan in the bread machine and close the lid.
**2. Select the Bake cycle**
Close the lid, Turn on the bread maker. Select the White / Basic setting, then select the dough size, select light or medium crust. Press start to start the cycle.
When this is done, and the bread is baked, remove the pan from the machine. Let stand a few minutes. Remove the bread from the skillet and leave it on a wire rack to cool for at least 10 minutes. Slice and serve.

# Whole Wheat Sunflower Bread

**PREP: 10 MINUTES /MAKES 1 LOAF**

**Ingredients**
- 12 slice bread (1½ pounds)
- 1 cup lukewarm water
- 1½ tablespoons honey
- 1½ tablespoons unsalted butter, melted
- ¾ teaspoon table salt
- 2½ cups whole-wheat flour
- ¾ cup white bread flour
- 1 tablespoon sesame seeds
- 3 tablespoons raw sunflower seeds
- 1½ teaspoons bread machine yeast

**Directions**
**1. Preparing the Ingredients.**
Measure and add the ingredients to the pan in the order mentioned above. Place the pan in the bread machine and close the lid.
**2. Select the Bake cycle**
Close the lid, Turn on the bread maker. Select the White / Basic setting, then select the dough size, select light or medium crust. Press start to start the cycle.
When this is done, and the bread is baked, remove the pan from the machine. Let stand a few minutes. Remove the bread from the pan and leave it on a wire rack to cool for at least 10 minutes. Slice and serve.

# Chocolate Chip Banana Bread

**PREP: 10 MINUTES /MAKES 1 LOAF**

**Ingredients**
- Shortening or gluten-free cooking spray, for preparing the pan
- 250 grams All-Purpose Flour Blend

- 1 teaspoon ground cinnamon
- 1 teaspoon xanthan gum
- 1 teaspoon baking powder
- ½ teaspoon baking soda
- ¼ teaspoon salt
- 2 large eggs
- 1 teaspoon vanilla extract
- 90 grams mini semisweet chocolate chips or nondairy alternative
- 80 grams plain Greek yogurt or nondairy alternative
- 450 grams mashed bananas (about 4 large bananas)
- 8 tablespoons (1 stick) butter or nondairy alternative
- 150 grams light brown sugar

**Directions**

**1. Preparing the Ingredients.**

Measure and add the ingredients to the pan in the order mentioned above. Place the pan in the bread machine and close the lid.

**2. Select the Bake cycle**

Close the lid, Turn on the bread maker. Select the White / Basic setting, then select the dough size, select light or medium crust. Press start to start the cycle.

When this is done, and the bread is baked, remove the pan from the machine. Let the bread cool in the pan for at least 20 minutes, then gently transfer it to a wire rack to cool completely

# Honey Sunflower Bread

**PREP: 10 MINUTES /MAKES 1 LOAF**

**Ingredients**
- 12 slice bread (1½ pounds)
- 1 cup lukewarm water
- 1 egg, at room temperature
- 3 tablespoons unsalted butter, melted
- 3 tablespoons skim milk powder
- 1½ tablespoons honey
- 1½ teaspoons table salt
- 3 cups white bread flour
- 1 teaspoon bread machine yeast
- ¾ cup raw sunflower seeds

**Directions**

**1. Preparing the Ingredients.**

Measure and add the ingredients to the pan in the order mentioned above. Place the pan in the bread machine and close the lid.

**2. Select the Bake cycle**

Close the lid, Turn on the bread maker. Select the White / Basic setting, then select the dough size, select light or medium crust. Press start to start the cycle.

When this is done, and the bread is baked, remove the pan from the machine. Let stand a few minutes. Remove the bread from the pan and leave it on a wire rack to cool for at least 10 minutes. Slice and serve.

# Flaxseed Milk Bread

**PREP: 10 MINUTES /MAKES 1 LOAF**

## Ingredients

- 16 slice bread (2 pounds)
- 1½ cups lukewarm milk
- 2 tablespoons unsalted butter, melted
- 2 tablespoons honey
- 2 teaspoons table salt
- 4 cups white bread flour
- ½ cup flaxseed
- 1½ teaspoons bread machine yeast

## Directions
**1. Preparing the Ingredients.**
Measure and add the ingredients to the pan in the order mentioned above. Place the pan in the bread machine and close the lid.
**2. Select the Bake cycle**
Close the lid, Turn on the bread maker. Select the White / Basic setting, then select the dough size, select light or medium crust. Press start to start the cycle.
When this is done, and the bread is baked, remove the pan from the machine. Let stand a few minutes. Remove the bread from the pan and leave it on a wire rack to cool for at least 10 minutes. Slice and serve.

# Honey Wheat Bread

**PREP: 10 MINUTES /MAKES 1 LOAF**

## Ingredients
- 16 slice bread (2 pounds)
- 1⅔ cups boiling water
- ¼ cup + 4 teaspoons cracked wheat
- ¼ cup unsalted butter, melted
- 3 tablespoons honey
- 1½ teaspoons table salt
- 1 cup whole-wheat flour
- 2 cups white bread flour
- 2 teaspoons bread machine yeast

## Directions
**1. Preparing the Ingredients.**
Measure and add the ingredients to the pan in the order mentioned above. Add the boiling water and

cracked wheat to the bread pan; set aside for 25–30 minutes for the wheat to soften. Place the pan in the bread machine and close the lid.

**2. Select the Bake cycle**

Close the lid, Turn on the bread maker. Select the White / Basic setting, then select the dough size, select light or medium crust. Press start to start the cycle.

When this is done, and the bread is baked, remove the pan from the machine. Let stand a few minutes. Remove the bread from the pan and leave it on a wire rack to cool for at least 10 minutes. Slice and serve.

# Toasted Almond Whole Wheat Bread

**PREP: 10 MINUTES /MAKES 1 LOAF**

## Ingredients

- 1 cup, plus 2 tablespoons water
- 3 tablespoons agave nectar
- 2 tablespoons butter, unsalted
- 1 1/2 cups bread flour
- 1 1/2 cups whole wheat flour
- 1/4 cup slivered almonds, toasted
- 1 teaspoon salt
- 1 1/2 teaspoons quick active dry yeast

## Directions

**1. Preparing the Ingredients**

Add all of the ingredients in bread machine pan in the order they appear above, reserving yeast. Make a well in the center of the dry ingredients and add the yeast.

**2. Select the Bake cycle**

Select the Basic cycle, light or medium crust color, and press Start. Remove baked bread from pan and cool on a rack before slicing.

# Bagels

**PREP: 10 MINUTES /MAKES 9**

## Ingredients

- 1 cup warm water
- 1 1/2 teaspoons salt
- 2 tablespoons sugar
- 3 cups bread flour
- 2 1/4 teaspoons active dry yeast
- 3 quarts boiling water
- 3 tablespoons white sugar
- 1 tablespoon cornmeal
- 1 egg white
- Flour, for surface

## Directions

**1. Preparing the Ingredients**

Place in the bread machine pan in the following order: warm water, salt, sugar, and flour.

Make a well in the center of the dry ingredients and add the yeast.

**2.   Select the Bake cycle**

Select Dough cycle and press Start.

When Dough cycle is complete, remove pan and let dough rest on a lightly floured surface. Stir 3 tablespoons of sugar into the boiling water.

Cut dough into 9 equal pieces and roll each piece into a small ball. Flatten each ball with the palm of your hand. Poke a hole in the middle of each using your thumb. Twirl the dough on your finger to make the hole bigger, while evening out the dough around the hole. Sprinkle an ungreased baking sheet with 1 teaspoon cornmeal. Place the bagel on the baking sheet and repeat until all bagels are formed.

Cover the shaped bagels with a clean kitchen towel and let rise for 10 minutes.

Preheat an oven to 375°F.

Carefully transfer the bagels, one by one, to the boiling water. Boil for 1 minute, turning halfway. Drain on a clean towel. Arrange  boiled bagels on the baking sheet. Glaze the tops with egg white and sprinkle any toppings you desire.

Bake for 20 to 25 minutes or until golden brown. Let cool on a wire rack before serving.

# Cracked Wheat Bread

**PREP: 10 MINUTES /MAKES 10 SLICES**

## Ingredients

* 1 1/4 cup plus 1 tablespoon water
* 2 tablespoons vegetable oil
* 3 cups bread flour
* 3/4 cup cracked wheat
* 1 1/2 teaspoons salt
* 2 tablespoons sugar
* 2 1/4 teaspoons active dry yeast

## Directions

**1.   Preparing the Ingredients**

Bring water to a boil.

Place cracked wheat in small mixing bowl, pour water over it and stir. Cool to 80°F. Place cracked wheat mixture into pan, followed by all ingredients (except yeast) in the order listed. Make a well in the center of the dry ingredients and add the yeast.

**2.   Select the Bake cycle**

Select the Basic Bread cycle, medium color crust, and press Start.

Check dough consistency after 5 minutes of kneading. The dough should be a soft, tacky ball. If it is dry and stiff, add water one 1/2 tablespoon at a time until sticky. If it's too wet and sticky, add 1 tablespoon of flour at a time.

Remove bread when cycle is finished and allow to cool before serving.

# Gluten-Free Whole Grain Bread

**PREP: 15 MINUTES /MAKES 12 SLICES**

## Ingredients

* 2/3 cup sorghum flour
* 1/2 cup buckwheat flour

- 1/2 cup millet flour
- 3/4 cup potato starch
- 2 1/4 teaspoons xanthan gum
- 1 1/4 teaspoons salt
- 3/4 cup skim milk
- 1/2 cup water
- 1 tablespoon instant yeast
- 5 teaspoons agave nectar, separated
- 1 large egg, lightly beaten
- 4 tablespoons extra virgin olive oil
- 1/2 teaspoon cider vinegar
- 1 tablespoon poppy seeds

## Directions

### 1. Preparing the Ingredients

Whisk sorghum, buckwheat, millet, potato starch, xanthan gum, and sea salt in a bowl and set aside.

Combine milk and water in a glass measuring cup. Heat to between 110°F and 120°F; add 2 teaspoons of agave nectar and yeast and stir to combine. Cover and set aside for a few minutes.

Combine the egg, olive oil, remaining agave, and vinegar in another mixing bowl; add yeast and milk mixture. Pour wet ingredients into the bottom of your bread maker. Top with dry ingredients.

### 2. Select the Bake cycle

Select Gluten-Free cycle, light color crust, and press Start.

After second kneading cycle sprinkle with poppy seeds.

Remove pan from bread machine. Leave the loaf in the pan for about 5 minutes before cooling on a rack. Enjoy!

# 50/50 Bread

**PREP: 15 MINUTES /MAKES 12 SLICES**

## Ingredients

- 1 Pound loaf
- ½ cup Lukewarm water
- ½ tbsp Honey
- 1 tbsp Unsalted butter, diced
- ¾ cup Plain bread flour
- ¾ cup  Whole wheat flour
- ¾ tbsp Brown sugar
- ¾ tbsp  Powdered milk
- ¾ tsp Salt
- ½ tsp Instant dry yeast

## Directions

### 1. Preparing the Ingredients

Add the ingredients into the bread machine as per the order of the ingredients listed above or follow your bread machine's instruction manual.

### 2. Select the Bake cycle

Select the whole-wheat setting and medium crust function.
When ready, turn the bread out onto a drying rack and allow it to cool, then serve.

# SOURDOUGH BREADS
## Simple Sourdough Starter
**PREP: 10 MINUTES PLUS FERMENTING TIME**

**MAKES 2 CUPS (32 SERVINGS)**

## Ingredients

- 2½ teaspoons active dry yeast
- 2 cups water, at 100°F to 110°F
- 2 cups all-purpose flour

## Directions
**1. Preparing the Ingredients.**

In a large nonmetallic bowl, stir together the yeast, water, and flour. Cover the bowl loosely and place it in a warm place to ferment for 4 to 8 days, stirring several times per day.

**2. Select the Bake cycle**

When the starter is bubbly and has a pleasant sour smell, it is ready to use.

Store the starter covered in the refrigerator until you wish to use it.

## Classic White Bread
**PREP: 10 MINUTES /MAKES 1 LOAF**

## Ingredients

- 12 slice bread (1½ pounds)
- 1¼ cup lukewarm water
- 3 tablespoons canola oil
- ¾ teaspoon apple cider vinegar
- 2 eggs, room temperature, slightly beaten
- 1½ cups white rice flour
- ⅔ cup tapioca flour
- ½ cup nonfat dry milk powder
- ½ cup potato starch
- ⅓ cup cornstarch
- 2 tablespoon sugar
- ⅔ tablespoon xanthan gum
- ⅔ teaspoon table salt
- 1¼ teaspoons bread machine yeast

## Directions
**1. Preparing the Ingredients.**

Choose the size of loaf of your preference and then measure the ingredients.

Add all of the ingredients mentioned previously in the list, close the lid after placing the pan in the bread machine.

**2. Select the Bake cycle**

Turn on the bread machine. Select the White/Basic setting, select the loaf size, and the crust color. Press start.

When the cycle is finished, carefully remove the pan from the bread maker and let it rest.

Remove the bread from the pan, put in a wire rack to cool for at least 10 minutes, and slice.

# No-Yeast Sourdough Starter

**PREP: 10 MINUTES PLUS FERMENTING TIME**

**MAKES 4 CUPS**

## Ingredients

- 2 cups all-purpose flour
- 2 cups chlorine-free bottled water, at room temperature

## Directions

**1. Preparing the Ingredients.**

Stir together the flour and water in a large glass bowl with a wooden spoon. Loosely cover the bowl with plastic wrap and place it in a warm area for 3 to 4 days, stirring at least twice a day, or until bubbly.

**2. Select the Bake cycle**

Store the starter in the refrigerator in a covered glass jar, and stir it before using.

Replenish your starter by adding back the same amount you removed, in equal parts flour and water.

# Potica

**PREP: 20 MINUTES/ MAKES 10 SERVINGS**

## Ingredients

- Bread dough
- ½ cup milk
- ¼ cup cold butter, cut into small pieces
- 1 egg
- 2 cups bread flour
- ¼ cup sugar
- ¼ teaspoon salt
- 1 teaspoon bread machine yeast or fast-acting dry yeast filling
- 2 cups finely chopped or ground walnuts (about 7 oz)
- 1/3 cup honey
- 1/3 cup milk
- 3 tablespoons sugar
- 1 egg white, beaten

## Directions

**1. Preparing the Ingredients.**

Measure carefully, placing all bread dough ingredients in bread machine pan in the order recommended by the manufacturer.

**2. Select the Bake cycle**

Select Dough/Manual cycle. Do not use delay cycle. Remove dough from pan, using lightly floured hands. Cover and let rest 10 minutes on lightly floured surface. In small saucepan, combine all filling ingredients except egg white. Bring to a boil over medium heat, stirring frequently. Reduce heat; simmer uncovered 5 minutes, stirring occasionally.

Spread in shallow dish; cover and refrigerate until chilled.

Grease large cookie sheet with shortening. Roll dough into 16×12-inch rectangle on lightly floured surface. Spread filling over dough to within ½ inch of edges. Starting with 16-inch side, roll up tightly; pinch seam to seal. Stretch and shape roll until even. Coil roll of dough to form a snail shape. Place on cookie sheet. Cover and let rise in warm place 30 to 60 minutes or until doubled in size. Dough is ready if indentation remains when touched.

Heat oven to 325°F. Brush egg white over dough. Bake 45 to 55 minutes or until golden brown. Remove from cookie sheet to cooling rack.

# Pecan Apple Spice Bread

**PREP: 10 MINUTES /MAKES 1 LOAF**

## Ingredients

- 12 slice bread (1½ pounds)
- ⅓ cup lukewarm water
- 2¼ tablespoons canola oil
- ¾ teaspoon apple cider vinegar
- 2¼ tablespoons light brown sugar, packed
- ¾ cup Granny Smith apples, grated
- 2 eggs, room temperature, slightly beaten
- ½ cup nonfat dry milk powder
- ½ cup brown rice flour
- ½ cup tapioca flour
- ½ cup millet flour
- ⅓ cup corn starch
- 1½ tablespoons apple pie spice
- ¾ tablespoon xanthan gum
- ¾ teaspoon table salt
- 1¼ teaspoons bread machine yeast
- ⅓ cup pecans, chopped

## Directions

**1. Preparing the Ingredients.**

Choose the size of loaf of your preference and then measure the ingredients.

Add all of the ingredients mentioned previously in the list, close the lid after placing the pan in the bread machine.

**2. Select the Bake cycle**

Turn on the bread machine. Select the White/Basic setting, select the loaf size, and the crust color. Press start.

When the cycle is finished, carefully remove the pan from the bread maker and let rest. When the machine signals to add ingredients, add the chopped pecans.

Remove the bread from the pan, put in a wire rack to cool for at least 10 minutes, and slice.

# No-Yeast Whole-Wheat Sourdough Starter

**PREP: 10 MINUTES PLUS FERMENTING TIME**

**MAKES 2 CUPS (32 SERVINGS)**

**Ingredients**
- 1 cup whole-wheat flour, divided
- ½ teaspoon honey
- 1 cup chlorine-free bottled water, at room temperature, divided

**Directions**
**1. Preparing the Ingredients.**
Stir together ½ cup of flour, ½ cup of water, and the honey in a large glass bowl with a wooden spoon. Loosely cover the bowl with plastic wrap and place it in a warm area for 5 days, stirring at least twice a day. After 5 days, stir in the remaining ½ cup of flour and ½ cup of water.
**2. Select the Bake cycle**
Cover the bowl loosely again with plastic wrap and place it in a warm area.
When the starter has bubbles and foam on top, it is ready to use.
Store the starter in the refrigerator in a covered glass jar, and stir it before using. If you use half, replenish the starter with ½ cup flour and ½ cup water

# Pumpkin Jalapeno Bread
**PREP: 10 MINUTES /MAKES 1 LOAF**

**Ingredients**
- 12 slice bread (1½ pounds)
- ½ cup lukewarm water
- 2 medium eggs, beaten
- ⅓ cup pumpkin puree
- 2¼ tablespoons honey
- 1½ tablespoons vegetable oil
- ¾ teaspoon apple cider vinegar
- 1½ teaspoons sugar
- ¾ teaspoon table salt
- ½ cup brown rice flour
- ½ cup tapioca flour
- ⅓ cup corn starch
- ⅓ cup yellow cornmeal
- ¾ tablespoon xanthan gum
- 1 small jalapeno pepper, seeded and deveined
- 1½ teaspoons crushed red pepper flakes
- 1¼ teaspoons bread machine yeast

**Directions**
**1. Preparing the Ingredients.**
Choose the size of loaf of your preference and then measure the ingredients.
Add all of the ingredients mentioned previously in the list, close the lid after placing the pan in the bread machine.
**2. Select the Bake cycle**
Turn on the bread machine. Select the White/Basic setting, select the loaf size, and the crust color. Press start.
When the cycle is finished, carefully remove the pan from the bread maker and let rest. When the

machine signals to add ingredients, add the chopped pecans.

Remove the bread from the pan, put in a wire rack to cool for at least 10 minutes, and slice.

# Basic Sourdough Bread

**PREP: 10 MINUTES /MAKES 1 LOAF**

## Ingredients

- 12 slice bread (1½ pounds)
- 2 cups Simple Sourdough Starter (here), fed, active, and at room temperature
- 2 tablespoons water, at 80°F to 90°F
- ¾ teaspoon apple cider vinegar
- 1⅓ teaspoons sugar
- 1 teaspoon salt
- 1⅔ cups white bread flour
- ½ cup nonfat dry milk powder
- 1 teaspoon bread machine or instant yeast

## Directions

**1. Preparing the Ingredients.**

Choose the size of loaf of your preference and then measure the ingredients.

Add all of the ingredients mentioned previously in the list, close the lid after placing the pan in the bread machine.

**2. Select the Bake cycle**

Turn on the bread machine. Select the White/Basic setting, select the loaf size, and the crust color. Press start.

When the cycle is finished, carefully remove the pan from the bread maker and let rest. When the machine signals to add ingredients, add the chopped pecans.

Remove the bread from the pan, put in a wire rack to cool for at least 5 minutes, and slice.

# Gluten-Free Sourdough Bread

**PREP: 5 MINUTES /MAKES 12**

## Ingredients

- 1 cup water
- 3 eggs
- 3/4 cup ricotta cheese
- 1/4 cup honey
- 1/4 cup vegetable oil
- 1 teaspoon cider vinegar
- 3/4 cup gluten-free sourdough starter
- 2 cups white rice flour
- 2/3 cup potato starch
- 1/3 cup tapioca flour
- 1/2 cup dry milk powder
- 3 1/2 teaspoons xanthan gum
- 1 1/2 teaspoons salt

**Directions**
**1.   Preparing the Ingredients.**
Combine wet ingredients and pour into bread maker pan.
Mix together dry ingredients in a large mixing bowl, and add on top of the wet ingredients.
**2.   Select the Bake cycle**
Select Gluten-Free cycle and press Start.
Remove the pan from the machine and allow the bread to remain in the pan for approximately 10 minutes.
Transfer to a cooling rack before slicing.

# Walnut Banana Bread

**PREP: 10 MINUTES /MAKES 1 LOAF**

**Ingredients**
- 12 slice bread (1½ pounds)
- ⅓ cup lukewarm water
- 2 tablespoons canola oil
- ¾ teaspoon apple cider vinegar
- 2 eggs, beaten
- 1½ small bananas, mashed
- ¾ teaspoon table salt
- ½ cup brown rice flour
- ½ cup white rice flour
- ½ cup amaranth flour
- ⅓ cup corn starch
- ¾ tablespoon xanthan gum
- ¾ teaspoon cinnamon
- ⅓ teaspoon nutmeg
- 1½ teaspoons bread machine yeast
- ¾ cup walnuts, chopped

**Directions**
**1.   Preparing the Ingredients.**
Choose the size of loaf of your preference and then measure the ingredients.
Add all of the ingredients mentioned previously in the list, close the lid after placing the pan in the bread machine.
**2.   Select the Bake cycle**
Turn on the bread machine. Select the Quick/Rapid setting, select the loaf size, and the crust color. Press start.
When the cycle is finished, carefully remove the pan from the bread maker and let it rest.
Remove the bread from the pan, put in a wire rack to cool for at least 10 minutes, and slice.

# Whole-Wheat Sourdough Bread

**PREP: 10 MINUTES /MAKES 1 LOAF**

**Ingredients**

- 12 slice bread (1½ pounds)
- ¾ cup plus 2 tablespoons water, at 80°F to 90°F
- ¾ cup plus 2 tablespoons No-Yeast Whole-Wheat Sourdough Starter (here), fed, active, and at room temperature
- 2 tablespoons melted butter, cooled
- 2 eggs, beaten
- 1 tablespoon sugar
- 1 teaspoon salt
- ½ cup brown rice flour
- 1½ teaspoons bread machine yeast
- ¾ cup walnuts, chopped

**Directions**
**1. Preparing the Ingredients.**
Choose the size of loaf of your preference and then measure the ingredients.
Add all of the ingredients mentioned previously in the list, close the lid after placing the pan in the bread machine.
**2. Select the Bake cycle**
Turn on the bread machine. Select the Wheat/Whole-Grain bread setting, select the loaf size, and the crust color. Press start. When the loaf is done, remove the bucket from the machine.
Let the loaf cool for 5 minutes. Gently shake the bucket to remove the loaf, and turn it out onto a rack to cool.

# Basic Honey Bread
**PREP: 10 MINUTES /MAKES 1 LOAF**

**Ingredients**
- 12 slice bread (1½ pounds)
- 1½ cups warm milk
- ¼ cup unsalted butter, melted
- 2 eggs, beaten
- 1 teaspoon apple cider vinegar
- ½ cup honey
- 1 teaspoon table salt
- 3 cups gluten-free flour(s) of your choice
- 1½ teaspoons xanthan gum
- 1¾ teaspoons bread machine yeast

**Directions**
**1. Preparing the Ingredients.**
Choose the size of loaf of your preference and then measure the ingredients.
Add all of the ingredients mentioned previously in the list, close the lid after placing the pan in the bread machine.
**2. Select the Bake cycle**
Turn on the bread machine. Select the White/Basic or Gluten-Free (if your machine has this setting) setting, select the loaf size, and the crust color. Press start.

When the cycle is finished, carefully remove the pan from the bread maker and let it rest.
Remove the bread from the pan, put in a wire rack to cool for at least 10 minutes, and slice.

# Multigrain Sourdough Bread

**PREP: 10 MINUTES /MAKES 1 LOAF**

## Ingredients
- 12 slice bread (1½ pounds)
- ⅔ cup water, at 80°F to 90°F
- ¾ cup Simple Sourdough Starter, fed, active, and at room temperature
- 2 tablespoons melted butter, cooled
- 2½ tablespoons sugar
- ¾ teaspoon salt
- ¾ cup multigrain cereal
- 2⅔ cups white bread flour
- 1½ teaspoons bread machine or instant yeast

## Directions
### 1. Preparing the Ingredients.
Choose the size of loaf of your preference and then measure the ingredients.
Add all of the ingredients mentioned previously in the list, close the lid after placing the pan in the bread machine.
### 2. Select the Bake cycle
Turn on the bread machine. Select the Wheat/Whole-Grain bread setting, select the loaf size, and the crust color. Press start. When the cycle is finished, carefully remove the pan from the bread maker and let it rest.
Remove the bread from the pan, put in a wire rack to cool for at least 10 minutes, and slice.

# Onion Buttermilk Bread

**PREP: 10 MINUTES /MAKES 1 LOAF**

## Ingredients
- 12 slice bread (1½ pounds)
- 1 cup lukewarm water
- 3 tablespoons unsalted butter, melted
- ¾ teaspoon apple cider vinegar
- 3 tablespoons dry buttermilk powder
- 3 medium eggs, beaten
- 3 tablespoons sugar
- 1 teaspoon table salt
- ⅓ cup potato flour
- ⅓ cup tapioca flour
- 1½ cups white rice flour
- ¾ tablespoon dill, chopped
- 3 tablespoons green onion, chopped
- 2⅔ teaspoons xanthan gum
- 1½ teaspoons bread machine yeast

**Directions**

**1. Preparing the Ingredients.**

Choose the size of loaf of your preference and then measure the ingredients.

Add all of the ingredients mentioned previously in the list, close the lid after placing the pan in the bread machine.

**2. Select the Bake cycle**

Turn on the bread machine. Select White/Basic or Gluten-Free (if your machine has this setting) setting, select the loaf size, and the crust color. Press start.

When the cycle is finished, carefully remove the pan from the bread maker and let it rest.

Remove the bread from the pan, put in a wire rack to cool for at least 10 minutes, and slice.

# Faux Sourdough Bread

**PREP: 10 MINUTES /MAKES 1 LOAF**

**Ingredients**

- 12 slice bread (1½ pounds)
- ¾ cup plus 1 tablespoon water, at 80°F to 90°F
- ⅓ cup sour cream, at room temperature
- 2¼ tablespoons melted butter, cooled
- 1½ tablespoons apple cider vinegar
- ¾ tablespoon sugar
- ¾ teaspoon salt
- 3 cups white bread flour
- 1 teaspoon bread machine or instant yeast

**Directions**

**1. Preparing the Ingredients.**

Choose the size of loaf of your preference and then measure the ingredients.

Add all of the ingredients mentioned previously in the list, close the lid after placing the pan in the bread machine.

**2. Select the Bake cycle**

Turn on the bread machine. Select the Wheat/Whole-Grain bread setting, select the loaf size, select medium crust color. Press start.

When the cycle is finished, carefully remove the pan from the bread maker and let it rest.

Remove the bread from the pan, put in a wire rack to cool for at least 10 minutes, and slice.

# Pecan Cranberry Bread

**PREP: 10 MINUTES /MAKES 1 LOAF**

**Ingredients**

- 12 slice bread (1½ pounds)
- 1⅛ cups lukewarm water
- 3 tablespoons canola oil
- ¾ tablespoon orange zest
- ¾ teaspoon apple cider vinegar
- 2 eggs, slightly beaten
- 2¼ tablespoons sugar

- ¾ teaspoon table salt
- 1½ cups white rice flour
- ½ cup nonfat dry milk powder
- ⅓ cup tapioca flour
- ⅓ cup potato starch
- ¼ cup corn starch
- ¾ tablespoon xanthan gum
- 1½ teaspoons bread machine yeast
- ½ cup dried cranberries
- ½ cup pecan pieces

**Directions**

**1. Preparing the Ingredients.**

Choose the size of loaf of your preference and then measure the ingredients.

2. Add all of the ingredients mentioned previously in the list, close the lid after placing the pan in the bread machine. **Select the Bake cycle**

Turn on the bread maker. Select the Gluten Free or Fruit/Nut (if your machine has this setting) setting, then the loaf size, and finally the crust color. Start the cycle. (If you don't have either of the above settings, use Basic/White.).

When the machine signals to add ingredients, add the pecans and cranberries. (Some machines have a fruit/nut hopper where you can add the pecans and cranberries when you start the machine. The machine will automatically add them to the dough during the baking process.).

When the cycle is finished, carefully remove the pan from the bread maker and let it rest.

Remove the bread from the pan, put in a wire rack to cool for at least 10 minutes, and slice.

# Sourdough Milk Bread

**PREP: 10 MINUTES /MAKES 1 LOAF**

## Ingredients

- 12 slice bread (1½ pounds)
- 1½ cups Simple Sourdough Starter (here) or No-Yeast Sourdough Starter (here), fed, active, and at room temperature
- ⅓ cup milk, at 80°F to 90°F
- 3 tablespoons olive oil
- 1½ tablespoons honey
- 1 teaspoon salt
- 3 cups white bread flour
- 1 teaspoon bread machine or instant yeast

**Directions**

**1. Preparing the Ingredients.**

Choose the size of loaf of your preference and then measure the ingredients.

Add all of the ingredients mentioned previously in the list, close the lid after placing the pan in the bread machine.

**2. Select the Bake cycle**

Turn on the bread machine. Select the White/Basic setting, select the loaf size, and the crust color. Press start.

When the cycle is finished, carefully remove the pan from the bread maker and let it rest.

Remove the bread from the pan, put in a wire rack to cool for at least 10 minutes, and slice.

# Cheese Potato Bread

**PREP: 10 MINUTES /MAKES 1 LOAF**

## Ingredients

- 12 slice bread (1½ pounds)
- 1 cup lukewarm water
- 2¼ tablespoons vegetable oil
- 2 large eggs, beaten
- ⅓ cup dry skim milk powder
- 3 tablespoons sugar
- ¾ teaspoon apple cider vinegar
- 1⅛ teaspoons table salt
- ⅓ cup cornstarch
- ½ cup cottage cheese
- 3 tablespoons snipped chives
- ⅓ cup instant potato buds
- ⅓ cup potato starch
- ⅓ cup tapioca flour
- 1½ cups white rice flour
- 1½ teaspoons bread machine yeast

**Directions**

**1. Preparing the Ingredients.**

Choose the size of loaf of your preference and then measure the ingredients.

Add all of the ingredients mentioned previously in the list, close the lid after placing the pan in the bread machine.

**2. Select the Bake cycle**

Turn on the bread machine. Select the White/ Basic or Gluten-Free (if your machine has this setting) setting, select the loaf size, and the crust color. Press start.

When the cycle is finished, carefully remove the pan from the bread maker and let it rest.

Remove the bread from the pan, put in a wire rack to cool for at least 10 minutes, and slice.

# Lemon Sourdough Bread

**PREP: 10 MINUTES /MAKES 1 LOAF**

## Ingredients

- 12 slice bread (1½ pounds)
- ¾ cup Simple Sourdough Starter (here) or No-Yeast Sourdough Starter (here), fed, active, and at room temperature
- ¾ cup water, at 80°F to 90°F
- 1 egg, at room temperature
- 3 tablespoons butter, melted and cooled
- ⅓ cup honey
- 1½ teaspoons salt
- 2 teaspoons lemon zest

- 1½ teaspoons lime zest
- ⅓ cup wheat germ
- 3 cups white bread flour
- 1¾ teaspoons bread machine or instant yeast

**Directions**

**1.  Preparing the Ingredients.**

Choose the size of loaf of your preference and then measure the ingredients.

2.  Add all of the ingredients mentioned previously in the list, close the lid after placing the pan in the bread machine **Select the Bake cycle** .

Turn on the bread machine. Select the Whole-Wheat/Whole-Grain bread setting, select the loaf size, select light or medium crust. Press start.

When the cycle is finished, carefully remove the pan from the bread maker and let it rest.

Remove the bread from the pan, put in a wire rack to cool for at least 10 minutes, and slice.

# Instant Cocoa Bread

**PREP: 10 MINUTES /MAKES 1 LOAF**

**Ingredients**
- 12 slice bread (1½ pounds)
- 1⅛ cups lukewarm water
- 2 large eggs, beaten
- 2¼ tablespoons molasses
- 1½ tablespoons canola oil
- ¾ teaspoon apple cider vinegar
- 2¼ tablespoons light brown sugar
- 1⅛ teaspoons table salt
- 1½ cups white rice flour
- ½ cup potato starch
- ¼ cup tapioca flour
- 1½ teaspoons xanthan gum
- 1½ teaspoons cocoa powder
- 1½ teaspoons instant coffee granules
- 2 teaspoons bread machine yeast

**Directions**

**1.  Preparing the Ingredients.**

Choose the size of loaf of your preference and then measure the ingredients.

2.  Add all of the ingredients mentioned previously in the list, close the lid after placing the pan in the bread machine **Select the Bake cycle**

Turn on the bread machine. Select the White/Basic or Gluten-Free (if your machine has this setting) setting, select the loaf size, select light or medium crust. Press start.

When the cycle is finished, carefully remove the pan from the bread maker and let it rest.

Remove the bread from the pan, put in a wire rack to cool for at least 10 minutes, and slice.

# San Francisco Sourdough Bread

## Ingredients

- 12 slice bread (1½ pounds)
- 1 cup plus 2 tablespoons Simple Sourdough Starter (here) or No-Yeast Sourdough Starter (here), fed, active, and at room temperature
- ½ cup plus 1 tablespoon water, at 80°F to 90°F
- 2¼ tablespoons olive oil
- 1½ teaspoons salt
- 2 tablespoons sugar
- 1½ tablespoons skim milk powder
- ⅓ cup whole-wheat flour
- 2⅔ cups white bread flour
- 1⅔ teaspoons bread machine or instant yeast

## Directions

### 1. Preparing the Ingredients.

Choose the size of loaf of your preference and then measure the ingredients.

Add all of the ingredients mentioned previously in the list, close the lid after placing the pan in the bread machine

### 2. Select the Bake cycle

Turn on the bread machine. Select the White/Basic setting, select the loaf size, and the crust color. Press start.

When the cycle is finished, carefully remove the pan from the bread maker and let it rest.

Remove the bread from the pan, put in a wire rack to cool for at least 10 minutes, and slice.

# Mix Seed Bread



## Ingredients

- 12 slice bread (1½ pounds)
- 2 cups lukewarm milk
- 6 tablespoons cooking oil
- 1 teaspoon vinegar
- 2 eggs, slightly beaten
- 1 tablespoon sugar
- 1 teaspoon table salt
- 2⅔ cups gluten-free flour(s) of your choice
- 2 tablespoons poppy seeds
- 2 tablespoons pumpkin seeds
- 2 tablespoons sunflower seeds
- 2 teaspoons bread machine yeast

## Directions

### 1. Preparing the Ingredients.

Choose the size of loaf of your preference and then measure the ingredients.

Add all of the ingredients mentioned previously in the list, close the lid after placing the pan in the bread machine

**2. Select the Bake cycle**

Turn on the bread machine. Select the White/Basic setting, select the loaf size, and the crust color. Press start.

When the cycle is finished, carefully remove the pan from the bread maker and let it rest.

Remove the bread from the pan, put in a wire rack to cool for at least 10 minutes, and slice.

# Sourdough Beer Bread

**PREP: 10 MINUTES /MAKES 1 LOAF**

## Ingredients

- 12 slice bread (1½ pounds)
- 1 cup Simple Sourdough Starter (here) or No-Yeast Sourdough Starter (here), fed, active, and at room temperature
- ½ cup plus 1 tablespoon dark beer, at 80°F to 90°F
- 1½ tablespoons melted butter, cooled
- ¾ tablespoon sugar
- 1⅛ teaspoons salt
- 2⅔ cups white bread flour
- 1⅛ teaspoons bread machine or instant yeast

**Directions**

**1. Preparing the Ingredients.**

Choose the size of loaf of your preference and then measure the ingredients.

Add all of the ingredients mentioned previously in the list, close the lid after placing the pan in the bread machine

**2. Select the Bake cycle**

Turn on the bread machine. Select the Wheat/Whole-Grain bread setting, select the loaf size, and the crust color. Press start.

When the cycle is finished, carefully remove the pan from the bread maker and let it rest.

Remove the bread from the pan, put in a wire rack to cool for at least 10 minutes, and slice.

# Garlic Parsley Bread

**PREP: 10 MINUTES /MAKES 1 LOAF**

## Ingredients

- 12 slice bread (1½ pounds)
- 1¼ cups almond or coconut milk
- 3 tablespoons flax meal
- ½ cup + 1 tablespoon warm water
- 3 tablespoons butter
- 2¼ tablespoons maple syrup
- 2¼ teaspoons apple cider vinegar
- 3 tablespoons parsley, loosely chopped
- 8–9 cloves garlic, minced
- ¾ teaspoon table salt
- 6 tablespoons + 2 teaspoons brown rice flour
- ⅓ cup corn starch

- 3 tablespoons potato starch
- 2 teaspoons xanthan gum
- 1½ tablespoons garlic powder
- 1½ tablespoons onion powder
- 1½ teaspoons bread machine yeast

## Directions
### 1. Preparing the Ingredients.
Combine the water and flax meal in a bowl; set aside for 5–10 minutes to mix well.

Choose the size of loaf of your preference and then measure the ingredients.

Add all of the ingredients mentioned previously in the list, including the flax meal. Close the lid after placing the pan in the bread machine.

### 2. Select the Bake cycle
Turn on the bread machine. Select the White/Basic or Gluten-Free (if your machine has this setting) setting, select the loaf size, select light or medium crust. Press start.

When the cycle is finished, carefully remove the pan from the bread maker and let it rest.

Remove the bread from the pan, put in a wire rack to cool for at least 10 minutes, and slice.

# Crusty Sourdough Bread

**PREP: 10 MINUTES /MAKES 1 LOAF**

## Ingredients
- 12 slice bread (1½ pounds)
- 1 cup Simple Sourdough Starter (here), fed, active, and at room temperature
- ½ cup water, at 80°F to 90°F
- 2 tablespoons honey
- 1½ teaspoons salt
- 3 cups white bread flour
- 1 teaspoon bread machine or instant yeast

## Directions
### 1. Preparing the Ingredients.
Choose the size of loaf of your preference and then measure the ingredients.

Add all of the ingredients mentioned previously in the list, close the lid after placing the pan in the bread machine

### 2. Select the Bake cycle
Turn on the bread machine. Select the Wheat/Whole-Grain bread setting, select the loaf size, and the crust color. Press start. When the cycle is finished, carefully remove the pan from the bread maker and let it rest.

Remove the bread from the pan, put in a wire rack to cool for at least 10 minutes, and slice.

# Italian Herb Bread

**PREP: 10 MINUTES /MAKES 1 LOAF**

## Ingredients
- 12 slice bread (1½ pounds)

- 1½ cups lukewarm water
- 3 eggs, beaten
- ¼ cup vegetable oil
- 1½ teaspoons table salt
- 3 tablespoons sugar
- 1 cup white bean flour
- 1 tablespoon mixed Italian herbs, dried
- 1 cup white rice flour
- 1 cup potato starch
- ½ cup tapioca flour
- 1 tablespoon xanthan gum
- 2¼ teaspoons bread machine yeast

**Directions**
**1. Preparing the Ingredients.**
Choose the size of loaf of your preference and then measure the ingredients.
Add all of the ingredients mentioned previously in the list, close the lid after placing the pan in the bread machine
**2. Select the Bake cycle**
Turn on the bread machine. Select the White/Basic or Gluten-Free (if your machine has this setting) setting, select the loaf size, select light or medium crust. Press start.
When the cycle is finished, carefully remove the pan from the bread maker and let it rest.
Remove the bread from the pan, put in a wire rack to cool for at least 10 minutes, and slice.

# Sourdough Cheddar Bread

**PREP: 10 MINUTES /MAKES 1 LOAF**

**Ingredients**
- 12 slice bread (1½ pounds)
- 1 cup Simple Sourdough Starter or No-Yeast Sourdough Starter, fed, active, and at room temperature
- ⅓ cup water, at 80°F to 90°F
- 4 teaspoons sugar
- 1 teaspoon salt
- ½ cup (2 ounces) grated aged Cheddar cheese
- ⅔ cup whole-wheat flour
- ¼ cup oat bran
- 1⅓ cups white bread flour
- 1½ teaspoons bread machine or instant yeast

**Directions**
**1. Preparing the Ingredients.**
Choose the size of loaf of your preference and then measure the ingredients.
Add all of the ingredients mentioned previously in the list, close the lid after placing the pan in the bread machine
**2. Select the Bake cycle**
Turn on the bread machine. Select the Wheat/Whole-Grain bread setting, select the loaf size, and the

crust color. Press start. When the cycle is finished, carefully remove the pan from the bread maker and let it rest.

Remove the bread from the pan, put in a wire rack to cool for at least 5 minutes, and slice.

# Herb Sourdough

**PREP: 10 MINUTES /MAKES 1 LOAF**

## Ingredients

- 8 slice bread (1 pound)
- 1⅓ cups No-Yeast Sourdough Starter, fed, active, and at room temperature
- 4 teaspoons water, at 80°F to 90°F
- 4 teaspoons melted butter, cooled
- 1⅓ teaspoons sugar
- 1 teaspoon salt
- 1 teaspoon chopped fresh basil
- 1 teaspoon chopped fresh oregano
- ½ teaspoon chopped fresh thyme
- 1⅔ cups white bread flour
- 1 teaspoon bread machine or instant yeast

## Directions

### 1. Preparing the Ingredients.

Choose the size of loaf of your preference and then measure the ingredients.

Add all of the ingredients mentioned previously in the list, close the lid after placing the pan in the bread machine

### 2. Select the Bake cycle

Turn on the bread machine. Select the Wheat/Whole-Grain bread setting, select the loaf size, and the crust color. Press start. When the cycle is finished, carefully remove the pan from the bread maker and let it rest.

Remove the bread from the pan, put in a wire rack to cool for at least 5 minutes, and slice

# Cranberry Pecan Sourdough

**PREP: 10 MINUTES /MAKES 1 LOAF**

## Ingredients

- 12 slice bread (1½ pounds)
- 2 cups No-Yeast Sourdough Starter (here), fed, active, and at room temperature
- 2 tablespoons water, at 80°F to 90°F
- 2 tablespoons melted butter, cooled
- 2 teaspoons sugar
- 1½ teaspoons salt
- ⅓ teaspoon ground cinnamon
- 2½ cups white bread flour
- 1½ teaspoons bread machine or instant yeast
- ⅓ cup dried cranberries
- ⅓ cup chopped pecans

**Directions**

**1. Preparing the Ingredients.**

Choose the size of loaf of your preference and then measure the ingredients.

Add all of the ingredients mentioned previously in the list, close the lid after placing the pan in the bread machine

**2. Select the Bake cycle**

Turn on the bread machine. Select the Wheat/Whole-Grain bread setting, select the loaf size, and the crust color. Press start. When the cycle is finished, carefully remove the pan from the bread maker and let it rest.

Remove the bread from the pan, put in a wire rack to cool for at least 5 minutes, and slice

# Dark Chocolate Sourdough

### PREP: 10 MINUTES /MAKES 1 LOAF

**Ingredients**

- 12 slice bread (1½ pounds)
- 2 cups No-Yeast Sourdough Starter, fed, active, and at room temperature
- 2 tablespoons water, at 80°F to 90°F
- 2 tablespoons melted butter, cooled
- ¾ teaspoon pure vanilla extract
- 2 teaspoons sugar
- 1½ teaspoons salt
- ⅓ teaspoon ground cinnamon
- ¼ cup unsweetened cocoa powder
- 2½ cups white bread flour
- 1½ teaspoons bread machine or instant yeast
- ½ cup semisweet chocolate chips
- ⅓ cup chopped pistachios
- ⅓ cup raisins

**Directions**

**1. Preparing the Ingredients.**

Choose the size of loaf of your preference and then measure the ingredients.

Add all of the ingredients mentioned previously in the list, close the lid after placing the pan in the bread machine

**2. Select the Bake cycle**

Turn on the bread machine. Select the Wheat/Whole-Grain bread setting, select the loaf size, and the crust color. Press start. When the cycle is finished, carefully remove the pan from the bread maker and let it rest.

Remove the bread from the pan, put in a wire rack to cool for at least 5 minutes, and slice

# FRUIT BREADS

## Cinnamon Apple Bread

## Ingredients

- 16 slice bread (2 pounds)
- 1⅓ cups lukewarm milk
- 3⅓ tablespoons butter, melted
- 2⅔ tablespoons sugar
- 2 teaspoons table salt
- 1⅓ teaspoons cinnamon, ground
- A pinch ground cloves
- 4 cups white bread flour
- 2¼ teaspoons bread machine yeast
- 1⅓ cups peeled apple, finely diced

## Directions

**1. Preparing the Ingredients.**

Choose the size of loaf of your preference and then measure the ingredients.

Add all of the ingredients mentioned previously in the list, except for the apples. Close the lid after placing the pan in the bread machine.

**2. Select the Bake cycle**

Turn on the bread machine. Select the White/Basic or Fruit/Nut (if your machine has this setting) setting, select the loaf size, and the crust color. Press start.

When the machine signals to add ingredients, add the apples.

When the cycle is finished, carefully remove the pan from the bread maker and let it rest.

Remove the bread from the pan, put in a wire rack to cool for at least 5 minutes, and slice

# Candied Fruits Bread

**PREP: 10 MINUTES /MAKES 1 LOAF**

## Ingredients

- Orange juice - 1 cup
- Lukewarm water - ½ cup
- Butter - 2½ tbsp., softened
- Powdered milk - 2 tbsp.
- Brown sugar - 2½ tbsp.
- Kosher salt - 1 tsp.
- Whole-grain flour - 4 cups
- Bread machine yeast - 1½ tsp.
- Candied fruits - ¾ cup (pineapple, coconut, papaya)
- Walnuts - ¼ cup, chopped
- All-purpose flour - 1 tbsp. for packing candied fruits
- Almond flakes - ¼ cup

## Directions

**1. Preparing the Ingredients**

Put the candied fruit water, then dry on a paper towel and roll in flour.

Choose the size of loaf of your preference and then measure the ingredients.

Add all of the ingredients mentioned previously in the list, (except almonds and fruit). Close the lid after placing the pan in the bread machine.

**2. Select the Bake cycle**

Turn on the bread machine. Select the Wheat/Whole-Grain bread setting, select the loaf size, and the crust color. Press start. When the cycle is finished, carefully remove the pan from the bread maker and let it rest.

Remove the bread from the pan, put in a wire rack to cool for at least 5 minutes, and slice.

# Banana Bread

**PREP: 10 MINUTES /MAKES 1 LOAF**

**Ingredients**

- 1¼ cups sugar
- ½ cup butter, softened
- 2 eggs
- 1½ cups mashed very ripe bananas (3 medium)
- ½ cup buttermilk
- 1 teaspoon vanilla
- 2½ cups all-purpose flour
- 1 teaspoon baking soda
- 1 teaspoon salt
- 1 cup chopped nuts, if desired

**Directions**

**1. Preparing the Ingredients.**

Place the banana, eggs, sugar, and vanilla in your bread machine. Choose the size of loaf of your preference and then measure the ingredients. Close the lid after placing the pan in the bread machine.

**2. Select the Bake cycle**

Program the machine for Quick/Rapid bread and press Start.

While the wet ingredients are mixing, stir together the flour, nuts, salt, and baking soda in a small bowl.

After the first fast mixing is done and the machine signals, add the dry ingredients.

When the cycle is finished, carefully remove the pan from the bread maker and let it rest.

Remove the bread from the pan, put in a wire rack to cool for at least 2 hours, and slice.

Wrap tightly and store at room temperature up to 4 days, or refrigerate.

# Blueberry Honey Bread

**PREP: 10 MINUTES /MAKES 1 LOAF**

**Ingredients**

- 16 slice bread (2 pounds)
- 1 cup plain yogurt
- ⅔ cup lukewarm water
- ¼ cup honey
- 4 teaspoons unsalted butter, melted
- 2 teaspoons table salt
- 1½ teaspoons lime zest
- ⅔ teaspoon lemon extract
- 4 cups white bread flour
- 2¼ teaspoons bread machine yeast
- 1⅓ cups dried blueberries

**Directions**

**1. Preparing the Ingredients.**

Choose the size of loaf of your preference and then measure the ingredients.

Add all of the ingredients mentioned previously in the list, except for the blueberries. Close the lid after placing the pan in the bread machine.

**2. Select the Bake cycle**

Turn on the bread machine. White/Basic or Fruit/Nut (if your machine has this setting) setting, select the loaf size, and the crust color. Press start.

When the machine signals to add ingredients, add the blueberries.

When the cycle is finished, carefully remove the pan from the bread maker and let it rest.

Remove the bread from the pan, put in a wire rack to cool for at least 10 minutes, and slice.

# Cranberry Orange Breakfast Bread

**PREP: 10 MINUTES /MAKES 14 SLICES**

**Ingredients**

- 1⅛ cup orange juice
- 2 Tbsp vegetable oil
- 2 Tbsp honey
- 3 cups bread flour
- 1 Tbsp dry milk powder
- ½ tsp ground cinnamon
- ½ tsp ground allspice
- 1 tsp salt
- 1 (.25 ounce) package active dry yeast
- 1 Tbsp grated orange zest
- 1 cup sweetened dried cranberries
- ⅓ cup chopped walnuts

**Directions**

**1. Preparing the Ingredients.**

Add each ingredient to the bread machine in the order and at the temperature recommended by your bread machine manufacturer.

**2. Select the Bake cycle**

Close the lid, select the basic bread, low crust setting on your bread machine, and press start.

Add the cranberries and chopped walnuts 5 to 10 minutes before last kneading cycle ends.

When the bread machine has finished baking, remove the bread and put it on a cooling rack.

# Chai-Spiced Bread

**PREP: 10 MINUTES /MAKES 1 LOAF**

**Ingredients**

- ¾ cup granulated sugar
- ½ cup butter, softened
- ½ cup cold brewed tea or water
- 1/3 cup milk
- 2 teaspoons vanilla
- 2 eggs

- 2 cups all-purpose flour
- 2 teaspoons baking powder
- ¾ teaspoon ground cardamom
- ½ teaspoon salt
- ¼ teaspoon ground cinnamon
- 1/8 teaspoon ground cloves
- glaze
- 1 cup powdered sugar
- ¼ teaspoon vanilla
- 3 to 5 teaspoons milk
- Additional ground cinnamon

**Directions**

**1. Preparing the Ingredients.**

Choose the size of loaf of your preference and then measure the ingredients.

Add all of the ingredients mentioned previously in the list. Close the lid after placing the pan in the bread machine.

**2. Select the Bake cycle**

Turn on the bread machine. Select the White/Basic setting, select the loaf size, and the crust color. Press start.

When the cycle is finished, carefully remove the pan from the bread maker and let it rest.

Remove the bread from the pan, put in a wire rack to cool for at least 2 hours, and slice. Wrap tightly and store at room temperature up to 4 days, or refrigerate.

# Raisin Candied Fruit Bread

**PREP: 10 MINUTES /MAKES 1 LOAF**

**Ingredients**
- 16 slice bread (2 pounds)
- 1 egg, beaten
- 1½ cups + 1 tablespoon lukewarm water
- ⅔ teaspoon ground cardamom
- 1¼ teaspoons table salt
- 2 tablespoons sugar
- ⅓ cup butter, melted
- 4 cups bread flour
- 1¼ teaspoons bread machine yeast
- ½ cup raisins
- ½ cup mixed candied fruit

**Directions**

**1. Preparing the Ingredients.**

Choose the size of loaf of your preference and then measure the ingredients.

Add all of the ingredients mentioned previously in the list, except for the candied fruits and raisins.

Close the lid after placing the pan in the bread machine.

**2. Select the Bake cycle**

Turn on the bread machine. White/Basic or Fruit/Nut (if your machine has this setting) setting, select the loaf size, and the crust color. Press start.

When the machine signals to add ingredients, add the candied fruits and raisins. When the cycle is finished, carefully remove the pan from the bread maker and let it rest.

Remove the bread from the pan, put in a wire rack to cool for at least 10 minutes, and slice.

# Strawberry Shortcake Bread

**PREP: 10 MINUTES /MAKES 1 LOAF**

## Ingredients

- 12 slice bread (1½ pounds)
- 1⅛ cups milk, at 80°F to 90°F
- 3 tablespoons melted butter, cooled
- 3 tablespoons sugar
- 1½ teaspoons salt
- ¾ cup sliced fresh strawberries
- 1 cup quick oats
- 2¼ cups white bread flour
- 1½ teaspoons bread machine or instant yeast

## Directions

**1. Preparing the Ingredients.**

Choose the size of loaf of your preference and then measure the ingredients.

Add all of the ingredients mentioned previously in the list. Close the lid after placing the pan in the bread machine.

**2. Select the Bake cycle**

Turn on the bread machine. Select the White/Basic setting, select the loaf size, and the crust color. Press start.

When the cycle is finished, carefully remove the pan from the bread maker and let it rest.

Remove the bread from the pan, put in a wire rack to cool for at least 2 hours, and slice.

# Chocolate-Pistachio Bread

**PREP: 10 MINUTES / MAKES 2⁄3 CUP (24 SLICES)**

## Ingredients

- 2⁄3 cup granulated sugar
- ½ cup butter, melted
- ¾ cup milk
- 1 egg
- 1½ cups all-purpose flour
- 1 cup chopped pistachio nuts
- ½ cup semisweet chocolate chips
- 1⁄3 cup unsweetened baking cocoa
- 2 teaspoons baking powder
- ¼ teaspoon salt
- Decorator sugar crystals, if desired

## Directions

**1. Preparing the Ingredients.**

Choose the size of loaf of your preference and then measure the ingredients.

Add all of the ingredients mentioned previously in the list. Close the lid after placing the pan in the bread machine.

**2.  Select the Bake cycle**

Turn on the bread machine. Select the White/Basic setting, select the loaf size, and the crust color. Press start.

When the cycle is finished, carefully remove the pan from the bread maker and let it rest.

Remove the bread from the pan, put in a wire rack to cool for at least 2 hours. Wrap tightly and store at room temperature up to 4 days, or refrigerate.

# Cinnamon-Raisin Bread

**PREP: 10 MINUTES / MAKES 14 SLICES**

**Ingredients**
- 1 cup water
- 2 Tbsp butter, softened
- 3 cups Gold Medal Better for Bread flour
- 3 Tbsp sugar
- 1½ tsp salt
- 1 tsp ground cinnamon
- 2½ tsp bread machine yeast
- ¾ cup raisins

**Directions**

**1.  Preparing the Ingredients**

Add each ingredient except the raisins to the bread machine in the order and at the temperature recommended by your bread machine manufacturer.

**2.  Select the Bake cycle**

Close the lid, select the sweet or basic bread, medium crust setting on your bread machine and press start.

Add raisins 10 minutes before the last kneading cycle ends.

When the bread machine has finished baking, remove the bread and put it on a cooling rack.

# Spice Peach Bread

**PREP: 10 MINUTES /MAKES 1 LOAF**

**Ingredients**
- 16 slice bread (2 pounds)
- ½ cup lukewarm heavy whipping cream
- 1 egg, beaten
- 1½ tablespoons unsalted butter, melted
- 3 tablespoons sugar
- 1½ teaspoons table salt
- ¼ teaspoon nutmeg, ground
- ½ teaspoon cinnamon, ground
- 3½ cups white bread flour
- ½ cup whole-wheat flour
- 1½ teaspoons bread machine yeast

- 1 cup canned peaches, drained and chopped

**Directions**
**1.    Preparing the Ingredients.**
Choose the size of loaf of your preference and then measure the ingredients.
Add all of the ingredients mentioned previously in the list, except for the peach. Close the lid after placing the pan in the bread machine.
**2.  Select the Bake cycle**
Turn on the bread machine. White/Basic or Fruit/Nut (if your machine has this setting) setting, select the loaf size, and the crust color. Press start.
When the machine signals to add ingredients, add the peaches. When the cycle is finished, carefully remove the pan from the bread maker and let it rest.
Remove the bread from the pan, put in a wire rack to cool for at least 10 minutes, and slice.

# Pineapple Coconut Bread

**PREP: 10 MINUTES /MAKES 1 LOAF**

**Ingredients**
- 6 tablespoons butter, at room temperature
- 2 eggs, at room temperature
- ½ cup coconut milk, at room temperature
- ½ cup pineapple juice, at room temperature
- 1 cup sugar
- 1½ teaspoons coconut extract
- 2 cups all-purpose flour
- ¾ cup shredded sweetened coconut
- 1 teaspoon baking powder
- ½ teaspoon salt

**Directions**
**1.  Preparing the Ingredients.**
Place the butter, eggs, coconut milk, pineapple juice, sugar, and coconut extract in your bread machine. Program the machine for Quick/Rapid bread and press Start.
While the wet ingredients are mixing, stir together the flour, coconut, baking powder, and salt in a small bowl.
**2.  Select the Bake cycle**
After the first fast mixing is done and the machine signals, add the dry ingredients.
When the cycle is finished, carefully remove the pan from the bread maker and let it rest.
Remove the bread from the pan, put in a wire rack to cool for at least 10 minutes, and slice.

# Chocolate-Cherry Bread

**PREP: 10 MINUTES /MAKES 1 LOAF**

**Ingredients**
- 1½ teaspoons baking powder
- ½ teaspoon baking soda
- ¼ teaspoon salt
- ¾ cup sugar

- ½ cup butter, softened
- 2 eggs
- 1 teaspoon almond extract
- 1 teaspoon vanilla
- 1 container (8 oz) sour cream
- ½ cup chopped dried cherries
- ½ cup bittersweet or dark chocolate chips

**Directions**

**1. Preparing the Ingredients.**

Choose the size of loaf of your preference and then measure the ingredients.

Add all of the ingredients mentioned previously in the list. Close the lid after placing the pan in the bread machine.

**2. Select the Bake cycle**

Turn on the bread machine. Select the White/Basic setting, select the loaf size, and the crust color. Press start.

When the cycle is finished, carefully remove the pan from the bread maker and let it rest.

Remove the bread from the pan, put in a wire rack to cool for at least 2 hours. Wrap tightly and store at room temperature up to 4 days, or refrigerate.

# Cocoa Date Bread

**PREP: 10 MINUTES /MAKES 1 LOAF**

**Ingredients**
- 12 slice bread (1½ pounds)
- ¾ cup lukewarm water
- ½ cup lukewarm milk
- 2 tablespoons unsalted butter, melted
- ¼ cup honey
- 3 tablespoons molasses
- 1 tablespoon sugar
- 2 tablespoons skim milk powder
- 1 teaspoon table salt
- 1¼ cups white bread flour
- 2¼ cups whole-wheat flour
- 1 tablespoon cocoa powder, unsweetened
- 1½ teaspoons bread machine yeast
- ¾ cup dates, chopped

**Directions**

**1. Preparing the Ingredients.**

Choose the size of loaf of your preference and then measure the ingredients.

Add all of the ingredients mentioned previously in the list, except for the dates. Close the lid after placing the pan in the bread machine.

**2. Select the Bake cycle**

Turn on the bread machine. White/Basic or Fruit/Nut (if your machine has this setting) setting, select the loaf size, and the crust color. Press start.

When the machine signals to add ingredients, add the dates. When the cycle is finished, carefully remove the pan from the bread maker and let it rest.

Remove the bread from the pan, put in a wire rack to cool for at least 10 minutes, and slice.

# Warm Spiced Pumpkin Bread

**PREP: 10 MINUTES /MAKES 1 LOAF**

**Ingredients**

- 12 to 16 slice bread (1½ to 2pounds)
- Butter for greasing the bucket
- 1½ cups pumpkin purée
- 3 eggs, at room temperature
- ⅓ cup melted butter, cooled
- 1 cup sugar
- 3 cups all-purpose flour
- 1½ teaspoons baking powder
- ¾ teaspoon ground cinnamon
- ½ teaspoon baking soda
- ¼ teaspoon ground nutmeg
- ¼ teaspoon ground ginger
- ¼ teaspoon salt
- Pinch ground cloves

**Directions**

1. **Preparing the Ingredients.**

Lightly grease the bread bucket with butter. Add the pumpkin, eggs, butter, and sugar.

2. **Select the Bake cycle.**

Program the machine for Quick/Rapid bread and press Start. Let the wet ingredients be mixed by the paddles until the first fast mixing cycle is finished, about 10 minutes into the cycle. While the wet ingredients are mixing, stir together the flour, baking powder, cinnamon, baking soda, nutmeg, ginger, salt, and cloves until well blended. Add the dry ingredients to the bucket when the second fast mixing cycle starts. Scrape down the sides of the bucket once after the dry ingredients are mixed into the wet. When the loaf is done, remove the bucket from the machine. Let the loaf cool for 5 minutes. Gently shake the bucket to remove the loaf, and turn it out onto a rack to cool.

# Ginger-Topped Pumpkin Bread

**PREP: 10 MINUTES / MAKES 2 LOAVES (24 SLICES EACH )**

**Ingredients**

- 1 can (15 oz) pumpkin (not pumpkin pie mix)
- 12/3 cups granulated sugar
- 2/3 cup unsweetened applesauce
- ½ cup milk
- 2 teaspoons vanilla
- 1 cup fat-free egg product or 2 eggs plus 4 egg whites 3 cups all-purpose flour
- 2 teaspoons baking soda
- 1 teaspoon salt
- 1 teaspoon ground cinnamon
- ½ teaspoon baking powder
- ½ teaspoon ground cloves

- glaze and topping
- 2/3 cup powdered sugar
- 2 to 3 teaspoons warm water
- ¼ teaspoon vanilla
- 3 tablespoons finely chopped crystallized ginger

**Directions**

**1. Preparing the Ingredients.**

Choose the size of loaf of your preference and then measure the ingredients.

Add all of the ingredients mentioned previously in the list. Close the lid after placing the pan in the bread machine.

**2. Select the Bake cycle**

Turn on the bread machine. Select the White/Basic setting, select the loaf size, and the crust color. Press start.

When the cycle is finished, carefully remove the pan from the bread maker and let it rest.

Remove the bread from the pan, put in a wire rack to cool for at least 2 hours. In small bowl, mix powdered sugar, water and ¼ teaspoon vanilla until thin enough to drizzle. Drizzle over loaves. Sprinkle with ginger. Wrap tightly and store at room temperature up to 4 days, or refrigerate up to 10 days.

# Strawberry Oat Bread

**PREP: 10 MINUTES /MAKES 1 LOAF**

**Ingredients**
- 16 slice bread (2 pounds)
- 1½ cups lukewarm milk
- ¼ cup unsalted butter, melted
- ¼ cup sugar
- 2 teaspoons table salt
- 1½ cups quick oats
- 3 cups white bread flour
- 2 teaspoons bread machine yeast
- 1 cup strawberries, sliced

**Directions**

**1.    Preparing the Ingredients.**

Choose the size of loaf of your preference and then measure the ingredients.

Add all of the ingredients mentioned previously in the list, except for the strawberries. Close the lid after placing the pan in the bread machine.

**2. Select the Bake cycle**

Turn on the bread machine. White/Basic or Fruit/Nut (if your machine has this setting) setting, select the loaf size, and the crust color. Press start.

When the machine signals to add ingredients, add the strawberries. When the cycle is finished, carefully remove the pan from the bread maker and let it rest.

Remove the bread from the pan, put in a wire rack to cool for at least 10 minutes, and slice.

# Black Olive Bread

**PREP: 10 MINUTES /MAKES 1 LOAF**

**Ingredients**
- 12 slices (1½ pounds)
- 1 cup milk, at 80°F to 90°F
- 1½ tablespoons melted butter, cooled
- 1 teaspoon minced garlic
- 1½ tablespoons sugar
- 1 teaspoon salt
- 3 cups white bread flour
- 1 teaspoon bread machine or instant yeast
- ⅓ cup chopped black olives

**Directions**

**1. Preparing the Ingredients.**

Choose the size of loaf of your preference and then measure the ingredients.

Add all of the ingredients mentioned previously in the list. Close the lid after placing the pan in the bread machine.

**2. Select the Bake cycle**

Turn on the bread machine. Select the White/Basic setting, select the loaf size, and the crust color. Press start.

When the cycle is finished, carefully remove the pan from the bread maker and let it rest.

Remove the bread from the pan, put in a wire rack to cool for at least 10 minutes.

# Cranberry & Golden Raisin Bread

**PREP: 10 MINUTES /MAKES 14 SLICES**

**Ingredients**
- 1⅓ cups water
- 4 Tbsp sliced butter
- 3 cups flour
- 1 cup old fashioned oatmeal
- ⅓ cup brown sugar
- 1 tsp salt
- 4 Tbsp dried cranberries
- 4 Tbsp golden raisins
- 2 tsp bread machine yeast

**Directions**

**1. Preparing the Ingredients**

Add each ingredient except cranberries and golden raisins to the bread machine one by one, according to the manufacturer's instructions.

**2. Select the Bake cycle**

Close the lid, select the sweet or basic bread, medium crust setting on your bread machine and press start.

Add the cranberries and golden raisins 5 to 10 minutes before the last kneading cycle ends.

When the bread machine has finished baking, remove the bread and put it on a cooling rack.

# Zucchini Bread

## Ingredients
- 3 cups shredded zucchini (2 to 3 medium)
- 1⅔ cups sugar
- ⅔ cup vegetable oil
- 2 teaspoons vanilla
- 4 eggs
- 3 cups all-purpose or whole wheat flour
- 2 teaspoons baking soda
- 1 teaspoon salt
- 1 teaspoon ground cinnamon
- ½ teaspoon baking powder
- ½ teaspoon ground cloves
- ½ cup chopped nuts
- ½ cup raisins, if desired

## Directions
**1. Preparing the Ingredients.**
Choose the size of loaf of your preference and then measure the ingredients.
Add all of the ingredients mentioned previously in the list. Close the lid after placing the pan in the bread machine.
**2. Select the Bake cycle**
Turn on the bread machine. Select the White/Basic setting, select the loaf size, and the crust color. Press start.
When the cycle is finished, carefully remove the pan from the bread maker and let it rest.
Remove the bread from the pan, put in a wire rack to cool for at least 2 hours before slicing. Wrap tightly and store at room temperature up to 4 days, or refrigerate up to 10 days.

# Cinnamon Figs Bread
**PREP: 10 MINUTES /MAKES 1 LOAF**

## Ingredients
- 16 slice bread (1½ pounds)
- 1⅛ cups lukewarm water
- 2¼ tablespoons unsalted butter, melted
- 3 tablespoons sugar
- ¾ teaspoon table salt
- ⅓ teaspoon cinnamon, ground
- ¾ teaspoon orange zest
- Pinch ground nutmeg
- 1⅞ cups whole-wheat flour
- 1⅛ cups white bread flour
- 1½ teaspoons bread machine yeast
- 1 cup chopped plums or sliced figs

## Directions
**1.  Preparing the Ingredients.**

Choose the size of loaf of your preference and then measure the ingredients.

Add all of the ingredients mentioned previously in the list, except for the plums. Close the lid after placing the pan in the bread machine.

**2. Select the Bake cycle**

Turn on the bread machine. White/Basic or Fruit/Nut (if your machine has this setting) setting, select the loaf size, and the crust color. Press start.

When the machine signals to add ingredients, add the plums. When the cycle is finished, carefully remove the pan from the bread maker and let it rest.

Remove the bread from the pan, put in a wire rack to cool for at least 10 minutes, and slice.

# Robust Date Bread

**PREP: 10 MINUTES /MAKES 1 LOAF**

## Ingredients

- 12 slice bread (1½ pounds)
- ¾ cup water, at 80°F to 90°F
- ½ cup milk, at 80°F
- 2 tablespoons melted butter, cooled
- ¼ cup honey
- 3 tablespoons molasses
- 1 tablespoon sugar
- 2 tablespoons skim milk powder
- 1 teaspoon salt
- 2¼ cups whole-wheat flour
- 1¼ cups white bread flour
- 1 tablespoon unsweetened cocoa powder
- 1½ teaspoons bread machine or instant yeast
- ¾ cup chopped dates

**Directions**

**1. Preparing the Ingredients.**

Choose the size of loaf of your preference and then measure the ingredients.

Add all of the ingredients mentioned previously in the list. Close the lid after placing the pan in the bread machine

**2. Select the Bake cycle**

Turn on the bread machine. Select the White/Basic setting, select the loaf size, and the crust color. Press start.

When the cycle is finished, carefully remove the pan from the bread maker and let it rest.

Remove the bread from the pan, put in a wire rack to cool for at least 10 minutes before slicing.

# Cranberry Honey Bread

**PREP: 10 MINUTES /MAKES 1 LOAF**

## Ingredients

- 16 slice bread (2 pounds)

- 1¼ cups + 1 tablespoon lukewarm water
- ¼ cup unsalted butter, melted
- 3 tablespoons honey or molasses
- 4 cups white bread flour
- ½ cup cornmeal
- 2 teaspoons table salt
- 2½ teaspoons bread machine yeast
- ¾ cup cranberries, dried

**Directions**

**1.    Preparing the Ingredients.**

Choose the size of loaf of your preference and then measure the ingredients.

Add all of the ingredients mentioned previously in the list. Close the lid after placing the pan in the bread machine

**2.  Select the Bake cycle**

Turn on the bread maker. Select the White/Basic or Fruit/Nut (if your machine has this setting) setting, then the loaf size, and finally the crust color. Start the cycle.

When the machine signals to add ingredients, add the dried cranberries.

When the cycle is finished and the bread is baked, carefully remove the pan from the machine. Use a potholder as the handle will be very hot. Let rest for a few minutes.

Remove the bread from the pan and allow to cool on a wire rack for at least 10 minutes before slicing.

# Apple Spice Bread

**PREP: 10 MINUTES /MAKES 1 LOAF**

**Ingredients**

- 16 slice bread (2 pounds)
- 1⅓ cup milk, at 80°F to 90°F
- 3⅓ tablespoons melted butter, cooled
- 2⅔ tablespoons sugar
- 2 teaspoons salt
- 1⅓ teaspoons ground cinnamon
- Pinch ground cloves
- 4 cups white bread flour
- 2¼ teaspoons bread machine or active dry yeast
- 1⅓ cups finely diced peeled apple

**Directions**

**1.  Preparing the Ingredients.**

Choose the size of loaf of your preference and then measure the ingredients.

Add all of the ingredients mentioned previously in the list, except for the apple. Close the lid after placing the pan in the bread machine.

**2.  Select the Bake cycle**

Turn on the bread machine. White/Basic or Fruit/Nut (if your machine has this setting) setting, select the loaf size, and the crust color. Press start.

When the machine signals to add ingredients, add the apple. When the cycle is finished, carefully remove the pan from the bread maker and let it rest.

Remove the bread from the pan, put in a wire rack to cool for at least 10 minutes, and slice.

# Poppy Seed–Lemon Bread

**PREP: 10 MINUTES /MAKES 1 LOAF**

## Ingredients

- 1 cup sugar
- ¼ cup grated lemon peel
- 1 cup milk
- ¾ cup vegetable oil
- 2 tablespoons poppy seed
- 2 teaspoons baking powder
- ½ teaspoon salt
- 2 eggs, slightly beaten

## Directions

### 1. Preparing the Ingredients.

Choose the size of loaf of your preference and then measure the ingredients.

Add all of the ingredients mentioned previously in the list. Close the lid after placing the pan in the bread machine

### 2. Select the Bake cycle

Turn on the bread machine. Select the White/Basic setting, select the loaf size, and the crust color. Press start.

When the cycle is finished, carefully remove the pan from the bread maker and let it rest.

Remove the bread from the pan, put in a wire rack to cool completely, about 2 hours. Wrap tightly and store at room temperature up to 4 days, or refrigerate.

# Ginger-Carrot-Nut Bread

**PREP: 10 MINUTES /MAKES 1 LOAF**

## Ingredients

- 2 eggs
- ¾ cup packed brown sugar
- 1/3 cup vegetable oil
- ½ cup milk
- 1 teaspoon vanilla
- 2 cups all-purpose flour
- 2 teaspoons baking powder
- 1 teaspoon ground ginger
- ½ teaspoon salt
- 1 cup shredded carrots (2 medium)
- ½ cup chopped nuts

## Directions

### 1. Preparing the Ingredients.

Choose the size of loaf of your preference and then measure the ingredients.

Add all of the ingredients mentioned previously in the list. Close the lid after placing the pan in the bread machine

### 2. Select the Bake cycle

Turn on the bread machine. Select the White/Basic setting, select the loaf size, and the crust color. Press

start.
When the cycle is finished, carefully remove the pan from the bread maker and let it rest.
Remove the bread from the pan, put in a wire rack to cool. Cool completely, about 10 minutes. Wrap tightly and store at room temperature up to 4 days, or refrigerate.

# Orange Bread

PREP: 10 MINUTES /MAKES 1 LOAF

**Ingredients**
- 16 slice bread (2 pounds)
- 1¼ cups lukewarm milk
- ¼ cup orange juice
- ¼ cup sugar
- 1½ tablespoons unsalted butter, melted
- 1¼ teaspoons table salt
- 4 cups white bread flour
- Zest of 1 orange
- 1¾ teaspoons bread machine yeast

**Directions**

**1. Preparing the Ingredients.**

Choose the size of loaf of your preference and then measure the ingredients.

Add all of the ingredients mentioned previously in the list. Close the lid after placing the pan in the bread machine

**2. Select the Bake cycle**

Turn on the bread machine. Select the White/Basic setting, select the loaf size, and the crust color. Press start.

When the cycle is finished, carefully remove the pan from the bread maker and let it rest.

Remove the bread from the pan, put in a wire rack to cool. Cool completely, about 10 minutes. Slice

# Lemon-Lime Blueberry Bread

PREP: 10 MINUTES /MAKES 1 LOAF

**Ingredients**
- 12 slice bread (1½ pounds)
- ¾ cup plain yogurt, at room temperature
- ½ cup water, at 80°F to 90°F
- 3 tablespoons honey
- 1 tablespoon melted butter, cooled
- 1½ teaspoons salt
- ½ teaspoon lemon extract
- 1 teaspoon lime zest
- 1 cup dried blueberries
- 3 cups white bread flour
- 2¼ teaspoons bread machine or instant yeast

**Directions**

**1. Preparing the Ingredients.**

Choose the size of loaf of your preference and then measure the ingredients.

Add all of the ingredients mentioned previously in the list. Close the lid after placing the pan in the bread machine

**2. Select the Bake cycle**

Turn on the bread machine. Select the White/Basic setting, select the loaf size, and the crust color. Press start.

When the cycle is finished, carefully remove the pan from the bread maker and let it rest.

Remove the bread from the pan, put in a wire rack to cool. Cool completely, about 10 minutes. Slice

# Apple-Fig Bread with Honey Glaze

**PREP: 10 MINUTES /MAKES 1 LOAF**

**Ingredients**

- 1½ cups all-purpose flour
- 1½ teaspoons ground cinnamon
- 1 teaspoon baking powder
- ½ teaspoon salt
- ½ teaspoon ground nutmeg
- ¼ teaspoon ground allspice
- 2/3 cup granulated sugar
- ½ cup vegetable oil
- 1 egg
- 1 egg yolk
- 1½ teaspoons vanilla
- ½ cup milk
- 1 cup chopped peeled apples
- ½ cup dried figs, chopped glaze
- 1/3 to ½ cup powdered sugar
- 2 tablespoons honey
- 1 tablespoon butter, softened
- Dash ground allspice

**Directions**

**1. Preparing the Ingredients.**

Choose the size of loaf of your preference and then measure the ingredients.

Add all of the ingredients mentioned previously in the list. Close the lid after placing the pan in the bread machine

**2. Select the Bake cycle**

Turn on the bread machine. Select the White/Basic setting, select the loaf size, and the crust color. Press start.

When the cycle is finished, carefully remove the pan from the bread maker and let it rest.

Remove the bread from the pan, put in a wire rack to cool. Cool completely, about 2 hours. In small bowl, beat 1/3 cup powdered sugar, the honey, butter and dash of allspice until smooth, slowly adding additional powdered sugar for desired glaze consistency. Spread glaze over top of loaf. Let stand until set. (Glaze will remain  slightly tacky to the touch.) Wrap tightly and store in refrigerator.

# Honey Banana Bread

**PREP: 10 MINUTES /MAKES 1 LOAF**

**Ingredients**
- 12 slice bread (1½ pounds)
- ½ cup lukewarm milk
- 1 cup banana, mashed
- 1 egg, beaten
- 1½ tablespoons unsalted butter, melted
- 3 tablespoons honey
- 1 teaspoon pure vanilla extract
- ½ teaspoon table salt
- 1 cup whole-wheat flour
- 1¼ cups white bread flour
- 1½ teaspoons bread machine yeast

**Directions**

**1. Preparing the Ingredients.**

Choose the size of loaf of your preference and then measure the ingredients.

Add all of the ingredients mentioned previously in the list. Close the lid after placing the pan in the bread machine

**2. Select the Bake cycle**

Turn on the bread maker. Select the Sweet setting, then the loaf size, and finally the crust color. Start the cycle.

When the cycle is finished and the bread is baked, carefully remove the pan from the machine.

Remove the bread from the pan and allow to cool on a wire rack for at least 10 minutes before slicing.

# Banana Whole-Wheat Bread

**PREP: 10 MINUTES /MAKES 1 LOAF**

**Ingredients**
- 12 slice bread (1½ pounds)
- ½ cup milk, at 80°F to 90°F
- 1 cup mashed banana
- 1 egg, at room temperature
- 1½ tablespoons melted butter, cooled
- 3 tablespoons honey
- 1 teaspoon pure vanilla extract
- ½ teaspoon salt
- 1 cup whole-wheat flour
- 1¼ cups white bread flour
- 1½ teaspoons bread machine or instant yeast

**Directions**

1. **Preparing the Ingredients.**

Choose the size of loaf of your preference and then measure the ingredients.

Add all of the ingredients mentioned previously in the list. Close the lid after placing the pan in the bread machine

2. **Select the Bake cycle.**

Turn on the bread machine. Select the Sweet bread setting, select the loaf size, and the crust color. Press start. When the cycle is finished, carefully remove the pan from the bread maker and let it rest. Shake the bucket to remove the loaf, and turn it out onto a rack to cool.

# Oatmeal-Streusel Bread

**PREP: 10 MINUTES /MAKES 1 LOAF**

**Ingredients**
**Streusel**
- ¼ cup packed brown sugar
- ¼ cup chopped walnuts, toasted
- 2 teaspoons ground cinnamon

**Bread**
- 1 cup all-purpose flour
- ½ cup whole wheat flour
- ½ cup old-fashioned oats
- 2 tablespoons ground flaxseed or flaxseed meal
- 1 teaspoon baking powder
- ½ teaspoon salt
- ¼ teaspoon baking soda
- ¾ cup packed brown sugar
- 2/3 cup vegetable oil
- 2 eggs
- ¼ cup sour cream
- 2 teaspoons vanilla
- ½ cup milk

**Icing**
- ¾ to 1 cup powdered sugar
- 1 tablespoon milk
- 2 teaspoons light corn syrup

**Directions**
**1.  Preparing the Ingredients .**
Choose the size of loaf of your preference and then measure the ingredients.
Add all of the ingredients mentioned previously in the list. Close the lid after placing the pan in the bread machine
**2.  Select the Bake cycle.**
Turn on the bread machine. Select the White/Basic setting, select the loaf size, and the crust color. Press start.
When the cycle is finished, carefully remove the pan from the bread maker and let it rest.
Remove the bread from the pan, put in a wire rack to Cool completely, about 2 hours.
In small bowl, beat all icing ingredients, adding enough of the powdered sugar for desired drizzling consistency. Drizzle icing over bread. Let stand until set. Wrap tightly and store at room temperature up to 4 days, or refrigerate. To toast walnuts, bake in ungreased shallow pan at 350°F for 7 to 11 minutes, stirring occasionally, until light brown.

# Garlic Olive Bread

**PREP: 10 MINUTES /MAKES 1 LOAF**

**Ingredients**

- 12 slice bread (1½ pounds)
- 1 cup lukewarm milk
- 1½ tablespoons unsalted butter, melted
- 1 teaspoon garlic, minced
- 1½ tablespoons sugar
- 1 teaspoon table salt
- 3 cups white bread flour
- 1 teaspoon bread machine yeast
- ⅓ cup black olives, chopped
- 16 slice bread (2 pounds)
- 1⅓ cups lukewarm milk
- 2 tablespoons unsalted butter, melted
- 1⅓ teaspoons garlic, minced
- 2 tablespoons sugar
- 1⅓ teaspoons table salt
- 4 cups white bread flour
- 1½ teaspoons bread machine yeast
- ½ cup black olives, chopped

**Directions**

**1. Preparing the Ingredients**

Choose the size of loaf of your preference and then measure the ingredients.

Add all of the ingredients mentioned previously in the list, except for the olives. Close the lid after placing the pan in the bread machine.

**2. Select the Bake**

Turn on the bread machine. White/Basic or Fruit/Nut (if your machine has this setting) setting, select the loaf size, and the crust color. Press start.

When the machine signals to add ingredients, add the olives. When the cycle is finished, carefully remove the pan from the bread maker and let it rest.

Remove the bread from the pan, put in a wire rack to cool for at least 10 minutes, and slice.

# Brown Bread with Raisins

**PREP: 10 MINUTES /MAKES 1 LOAF**

**Ingredients**

- 32 slices
- 1 cup all-purpose flour
- 1 cup whole wheat flour
- 1 cup whole-grain cornmeal
- 1 cup raisins
- 2 cups buttermilk
- ¾ cup molasses
- 2 teaspoons baking soda
- 1 teaspoon salt

**Directions**

**1. Preparing the Ingredients.**

Choose the size of loaf of your preference and then measure the ingredients.

Add all of the ingredients mentioned previously in the list. Close the lid after placing the pan in the bread machine.

**2.  Select the Bake cycle**

Turn on the bread machine. Select the White/Basic setting, select the loaf size, and the crust color. Press start.

When the cycle is finished, carefully remove the pan from the bread maker and let it rest.

Remove the bread from the pan, put in a wire rack to Cool completely, about 30 minutes.

# Cinnamon Pumpkin Bread

**PREP: 10 MINUTES /MAKES 1 LOAF**

**Ingredients**

- 16 slice bread (2 pounds)
- 2 cups pumpkin puree
- 4 eggs, slightly beaten
- ½ cup unsalted butter, melted
- 1¼ cups sugar
- ½ teaspoon table salt
- 4 cups white bread flour
- 1 teaspoon cinnamon, ground
- ¾ teaspoon baking soda
- ½ teaspoon nutmeg, ground
- ½ teaspoon ginger, ground
- Pinch ground cloves
- 2 teaspoons baking powder

**Directions**

**1.    Preparing the Ingredients.**

Choose the size of loaf of your preference and then measure the ingredients.

Add all of the ingredients mentioned previously in the list. Close the lid after placing the pan in the bread machine.

**2.  Select the Bake cycle**

Turn on the bread machine. Select the Quick/Rapid setting, select the loaf size, and the crust color. Press start.

When the cycle is finished, carefully remove the pan from the bread maker and let it rest.

Remove the bread from the pan, put in a wire rack to Cool completely, about 30 minutes. Slice

# Plum Orange Bread

**PREP: 10 MINUTES /MAKES 1 LOAF**

**Ingredients**

- 12 slice bread (1½ pounds)
- 1⅛ cup water, at 80°F to 90°F
- 2¼ tablespoons melted butter, cooled
- 3 tablespoons sugar
- ¾ teaspoon salt
- ¾ teaspoon orange zest

- ⅓ teaspoon ground cinnamon
- Pinch ground nutmeg
- 1¾ cups plus 2 tablespoons whole-wheat flour
- 1⅛ cups white bread flour
- 1½ teaspoons bread machine or instant yeast
- 1 cup chopped fresh plums

**Directions**

**1. Preparing the Ingredients.**

Choose the size of loaf of your preference and then measure the ingredients.

Add all of the ingredients mentioned previously in the list, except for the plums. Close the lid after placing the pan in the bread machine.

**2. Select the Bake cycle**

Turn on the bread machine. White/Basic or Fruit/Nut (if your machine has this setting) setting, select the loaf size, and the crust color. Press start.

When the machine signals to add ingredients, add the plums. When the cycle is finished, carefully remove the pan from the bread maker and let it rest.

Remove the bread from the pan, put in a wire rack to cool for at least 10 minutes, and slice.

# Blueberries 'n Orange Bread

**PREP: 10 MINUTES /MAKES 1 LOAF**

**Ingredients**

- 18 slices bread
- 3 cups Original Bisquick mix
- ½ cup granulated sugar
- 1 tablespoon grated orange peel
- ½ cup milk
- 3 tablespoons vegetable oil
- 2 eggs
- 1 cup fresh or frozen (rinsed and drained) blueberries glaze
- ½ cup powdered sugar
- 3 to 4 teaspoons orange juice
- Additional grated orange peel, if desired

**Directions**

**1. Preparing the Ingredients.**

Choose the size of loaf of your preference and then measure the ingredients.

Add all of the ingredients mentioned previously in the list. Close  the lid after placing the pan in the bread machine.

**2. Select the Bake cycle**

Program the machine for Basic/White bread, select light or medium crust, and press Start. When the loaf is done, remove the bucket from the machine. Let the loaf cool for 5 minutes.

Gently shake the bucket to remove the loaf, and turn it out onto a rack to cool. Cool completely, about 45 minutes.

In small bowl, mix powdered sugar and orange juice until smooth and thin enough to drizzle. Drizzle glaze over bread; sprinkle with additional orange peel.

# Peaches and Cream Bread

## Ingredients

- 12 slice bread (1½ pounds)
- ¾ cup canned peaches, drained and chopped
- ⅓ cup heavy whipping cream, at 80°F to 90°F
- 1 egg, at room temperature
- 1 tablespoon melted butter, cooled
- 2¼ tablespoons sugar
- 1⅛ teaspoons salt
- ⅓ teaspoon ground cinnamon
- ⅛ teaspoon ground nutmeg
- ⅓ cup whole-wheat flour
- 2⅔ cups white bread flour
- 1⅛ teaspoons bread machine or instant yeast

## Directions

### 1. Preparing the Ingredients.

Choose the size of loaf of your preference and then measure the ingredients.

Add all of the ingredients mentioned previously in the list. Close the lid after placing the pan in the bread machine.

### 2. Select the Bake cycle

Turn on the bread machine. Select the White/Basic setting, select the loaf size, and the crust color. Press start.

When the cycle is finished, carefully remove the pan from the  bread maker and let it rest.

Remove the bread from the pan, put in a wire rack to Cool completely, about 10 minutes.

# Gluten-Free Glazed Lemon-Pecan Bread



## Ingredients

- 12 slice bread (1½ pounds)
- ½ cup white rice flour
- ½ cup tapioca flour
- ½ cup potato starch
- ¼ cup sweet white sorghum flour
- ¼ cup garbanzo and fava flour
- 1 teaspoon xanthan gum
- 1 teaspoon gluten-free baking powder
- 1 teaspoon baking soda
- ½ teaspoon salt
- 2 eggs
- ½ cup sunflower or canola oil or melted ghee
- ¼ cup almond milk, soymilk or regular milk
- ½ teaspoon cider vinegar
- 1 tablespoon grated lemon peel
- ¼ cup fresh lemon juice
- 2/3 cup granulated sugar

- ½ cup chopped pecans
- glaze
- 2 tablespoons fresh lemon juice
- 1 cup gluten-free powdered sugar

**Directions**

1. **Preparing the Ingredients.**

Choose the size of loaf of your preference and then measure the ingredients.

Add all of the ingredients mentioned previously in the list. Close the lid after placing the pan in the bread machine.

2. **Select the Bake cycle.**

Turn on the bread machine. Select the White/Basic setting, select the loaf size, and the crust color. Press start. When the cycle is finished, carefully remove the pan from the bread maker and let it rest.

Remove the bread from the pan, put in a wire rack to Cool about 10 minutes.

In small bowl, stir all glaze ingredients until smooth. With fork, poke holes in top of loaf; drizzle glaze over loaf. Serve warm.

# Fresh Blueberry Bread

**PREP: 10 MINUTES /MAKES 1 LOAF**

**Ingredients**

- 12 to 16 slices (1½ to 2 pounds)
- 1 cup plain Greek yogurt, at room temperature
- ½ cup milk, at room temperature
- 3 tablespoons butter, at room temperature
- 2 eggs, at room temperature
- ½ cup sugar
- ¼ cup light brown sugar
- 1 teaspoon pure vanilla extract
- ½ teaspoon lemon zest
- 2 cups all-purpose flour
- 1 tablespoon baking powder
- ¾ teaspoon salt
- ¼ teaspoon ground nutmeg
- 1 cup blueberries

**Directions**

1. **Preparing the Ingredients.**

Place the yogurt, milk, butter, eggs, sugar, brown sugar, vanilla, and zest in your bread machine.

2. **Select the Bake cycle.**

Program the machine for Quick/Rapid bread and press Start. While the wet ingredients are mixing, stir together the flour, baking powder, salt, and nutmeg in a medium bowl. After the first fast mixing is done and the machine signals, add the dry ingredients. When the second mixing cycle is complete, stir in the blueberries. When the loaf is done, remove the bucket from the machine. Let the loaf cool for 5 minutes. Gently shake the bucket to remove the loaf, and turn it out onto a rack to cool.

# Gluten-Free Best-Ever Banana Bread

**PREP: 10 MINUTES /MAKES 1 LOAF**

**Ingredients**

- 16 slices bread

- ½ cup tapioca flour
- ½ cup white rice flour
- ½ cup potato starch
- ¼ cup garbanzo and fava flour
- ¼ cup sweet white sorghum flour
- 1 teaspoon xanthan gum
- ½ teaspoon guar gum
- 1 teaspoon gluten-free baking powder
- 1 teaspoon baking soda
- 1 teaspoon salt
- 1 teaspoon ground cinnamon
- ¾ cup packed brown sugar
- 1 cup mashed very ripe bananas (2 medium)
- ½ cup ghee (measured melted)
- ¼ cup almond milk, soymilk or regular milk
- 1 teaspoon gluten-free vanilla
- 2 eggs

**Directions**

**1. Preparing the Ingredients.**

Choose the size of loaf of your preference and then measure the ingredients. Add all of the ingredients mentioned previously in the list. Close the lid after placing the pan in the bread machine.

**2. Select the Bake cycle**

Turn on the bread machine. Select the White/Basic setting, select the loaf size, and the crust color. Press start.

When the cycle is finished, carefully remove the pan from the bread maker and let it rest. Remove the bread from the pan, put in a wire rack to Cool about 1 hour.

# Blueberry-Basil Loaf

**PREP: 10 MINUTES /MAKES 1 LOAF**

**Ingredients**
- 12 slice bread (1½ pounds)
- 1¼ cups fresh blueberries
- 1 tablespoon all-purpose flour
- 2¼ cups all-purpose flour
- 1 cup granulated sugar
- 2 teaspoons baking powder
- 1 teaspoon grated lemon peel
- ½ teaspoon salt
- 1 cup buttermilk
- 6 tablespoons butter, melted
- 1 teaspoon vanilla
- 2 eggs
- ¼ cup coarsely chopped fresh basil leaves
- Topping
- ½ cup packed brown sugar

- ¼ cup butter, melted
- 2/3 cup all-purpose flour

**Directions**
**1. Preparing the Ingredients.**
Choose the size of loaf of your preference and then measure the ingredients.
Add all of the ingredients mentioned previously in the list. Close the lid after placing the pan in the bread machine.
**2. Select the Bake cycle**
Turn on the bread machine. Select the White/Basic setting, select the loaf size, and the crust color. Press start.
When the cycle is finished, carefully remove the pan from the bread maker and let it rest.
Remove the bread from the pan, put in a wire rack to Cool about 1 hour.

# Savory Sweet Potato Pan Bread

**PREP: 10 MINUTES /MAKES 1 LOAF**

**Ingredients**
- 8 wedges
- 1½ cups uncooked shredded dark-orange sweet potato (about ½ potato) ½ cup sugar
- ¼ cup vegetable oil
- 2 eggs
- ¾ cup all-purpose flour
- ¾ cup whole wheat flour
- 2 teaspoons dried minced onion
- 1 teaspoon dried rosemary leaves, crumbled
- 1 teaspoon baking soda
- ½ teaspoon salt
- ¼ teaspoon baking powder
- 2 teaspoons sesame seed

**Directions**
**1. Preparing the Ingredients.**
Choose the size of loaf of your preference and then measure the ingredients.
Add all of the ingredients mentioned previously in the list. Close the lid after placing the pan in the bread machine.
**2. Select the Bake cycle**
Turn on the bread machine. Select the White/Basic setting, select the loaf size, and the crust color. Press start.
When the cycle is finished, carefully remove the pan from the bread maker and let it rest.
Remove the bread from the pan, put in a wire rack to Cool about 10 minutes. Serve warm.

# Cardamom Cranberry Bread

**PREP: 10 MINUTES /MAKES 1 LOAF**

**Ingredients**
- 1¾ cups water

- 2 Tbsp brown sugar
- 1½ tsp salt
- 2 Tbsp coconut oil
- 4 cups flour
- 2 tsp cinnamon
- 2 tsp cardamom
- 1 cup dried cranberries
- 2 tsp yeast

**Directions**

**1. Preparing the Ingredients**

Add each ingredient except the dried cranberries to the bread machine in the order and at the temperature recommended by your bread machine manufacturer.

**2. Select the Bake cycle**

Close the lid, select the basic bread, medium crust setting on your bread machine and press start. Add the dried cranberries 5 to 10 minutes before the last kneading cycle ends.

When the bread machine has finished baking, remove the bread and put it on a cooling rack.

# Rosemary Cranberry Pecan Bread

PREP: 10 MINUTES /MAKES 14 SLICES

**Ingredients**

- 1⅓ cups water, plus
- 2 Tbsp water
- 2 Tbsp butter
- 2 tsp salt
- 4 cups bread flour
- ¾ cup dried sweetened cranberries
- ¾ cup toasted chopped pecans
- 2 Tbsp non-fat powdered milk
- ¼ cup sugar
- 2 tsp yeast

**Directions**

**1. Preparing the Ingredients**

Add each ingredient to the bread machine in the order and at the temperature recommended by your bread machine manufacturer.

**2. Select the Bake cycle**

Close the lid, select the basic bread, medium crust setting on your bread machine and press start.

When the bread machine has finished baking, remove the bread and put it on a cooling rack .

# Harvest Fruit Bread

PREP: 10 MINUTES /MAKES 14 SLICES

**Ingredients**

- 1 cup plus 2 Tbsp water (70°F to 80°F)
- 1 egg
- 3 Tbsp butter, softened
- ¼ cup packed brown sugar

- 1½ tsp salt
- ¼ tsp ground nutmeg
- Dash allspice
- 3¾ cups plus 1 Tbsp bread flour
- 2 tsp active dry yeast
- 1 cup dried fruit (dried cherries, cranberries and/or raisins)
- ⅓ cup chopped pecans

**Directions**

**1. Preparing the Ingredients**

Add each ingredient except the fruit and pecans to the bread machine in the order and at the temperature recommended by your bread machine manufacturer.

**2. Select the Bake cycle**

Close the lid, select the basic bread, medium crust setting on your bread machine, and press start.

Just before the final kneading, add the fruit and pecans.

When the bread machine has finished baking, remove the bread and put it on a cooling rack.

# Cranberry Walnut Wheat Bread

**PREP: 10 MINUTES /MAKES 14 SLICES**

**Ingredients**

- 1 cup warm water
- 1 tablespoon molasses
- 2 tablespoons butter
- 1 teaspoon salt
- 2 cups 100% whole wheat flour
- 1 cup unbleached flour
- 2 tablespoons dry milk
- 1 cup cranberries
- 1 cup walnuts, chopped
- 2 teaspoons active dry yeast

**Directions**

**1. Preparing the Ingredients**

Add the liquid ingredients to the bread maker pan. Add the dry ingredients, except the yeast, walnuts and cranberries.

Make a well in the center of the bread flour and add the yeast. Insert the pan into your bread maker and secure the lid.

**2. Select the Bake cycle**

Select Wheat Bread setting, choose your preferred crust color, and press Start. Add cranberries and walnuts after first kneading cycle is finished. Remove the bread from the oven and turn it out of the pan onto a cooling rack and allow it to cool completely before slicing.

# Banana Split Loaf

**PREP: 10 MINUTES /MAKES 12 SLICES**

**Ingredients**

- 2 eggs

- 1/3 cup butter, melted
- 2 tablespoons whole milk
- 2 overripe bananas, mashed
- 2 cups all-purpose flour
- 2/3 cups sugar
- 1 1/4 teaspoons baking powder
- 1/2 teaspoon baking soda
- 1/2 teaspoon salt
- 1 cup chopped walnuts
- 1/2 cup chocolate chips

**Directions**

**1. Preparing the Ingredients**

Pour eggs, butter, milk and bananas into the bread maker pan and set aside.

Stir together all dry ingredients in a large mixing bowl.

Add dry ingredients to bread maker pan.

**2. Select the Bake cycle**

Set to Basic setting, medium crust color, and press Start.

Remove bread and place on a cooling rack before serving.

# Cranberry Orange Pecan Bread

**PREP: 5 MINUTES /MAKES 12 SLICES**

**Ingredients**

- 1 cup water
- 1/4 cup orange juice
- 2 teaspoons salt
- 1/3 cup sugar
- 2 1/2 tablespoons nonfat dry milk
- 2 1/2 tablespoons butter, cubed
- 4 cups bread flour
- 2 1/2 teaspoons orange zest
- 2 1/2 teaspoons bread machine yeast
- 1/2 cup dried cranberries
- 1/2 cup pecans, chopped

**Directions**

**1. Preparing the Ingredients**

Set aside cranberries and pecans, then place all other ingredients in the bread maker pan in order listed.

**2. Select the Bake cycle**

Choose Sweet cycle, light crust and press Start.

Add cranberries and pecans at the end of the kneading cycle.

Transfer to a plate and let cool 10 minutes before slicing with a bread knife.

# Pineapple Carrot Bread

**PREP: 5 MINUTES /MAKES 12 SLICES**

**Ingredients**

- 1 (8-ounce) can crushed pineapple, with juice
- 1/2 cup carrots, shredded
- 2 eggs
- 2 tablespoons butter
- 4 cups bread flour
- 3 tablespoons sugar
- 1 teaspoon salt
- 3/4 teaspoon ground ginger
- 1 1/4 teaspoons active dry yeast

**Directions**

**1. Preparing the Ingredients**

Add all of the ingredients (except yeast) to the bread maker pan in the order listed above.

Make a well in the center of the dry ingredients and add the yeast.

**2. Select the Bake cycle**

Select the Basic bread cycle and press Start.

Transfer baked loaf to a cooling rack for 15 minutes before slicing to serve.

# Gluten-Free Cinnamon Raisin Bread

PREP: 5 MINUTES /MAKES 12 SLICES

**Ingredients**

- 3/4 cup almond milk
- 2 tablespoons flax meal
- 6 tablespoons warm water
- 1 1/2 teaspoons apple cider vinegar
- 2 tablespoons butter
- 1 1/2 tablespoons honey
- 1 2/3 cups brown rice flour
- 1/4 cup corn starch
- 2 tablespoons potato starch
- 1 1/2 teaspoons xanthan gum
- 1 tablespoon cinnamon
- 1/2 teaspoon salt
- 1 teaspoon active dry yeast
- 1/2 cup raisins

**Directions**

**1. Preparing the Ingredients**

Mix together flax and water and let stand for 5 minutes.

Combine dry ingredients in a separate bowl, except for yeast.

Add wet ingredients to the bread machine.

Add the dry mixture on top and make a well in the middle of the dry mixture.

Add the yeast to the well.

**2. Select the Bake cycle**

Set to Gluten Free, light crust color, and press Start. After first kneading and rise cycle, add raisins.

Remove to a cooling rack when baked and let cool for 15 minutes before slicing.

# SPICE AND NUT BREAD

## Super Spice Bread

### PREP: 10 MINUTES /MAKES 1 LOAF

**Ingredients**
- 16 slice bread (2 pounds)
- 1⅓ cups lukewarm milk
- 2 eggs, at room temperature
- 2 tablespoons unsalted butter, melted
- 2⅔ tablespoons honey
- 1⅓ teaspoons table salt
- 4 cups white bread flour
- 1⅓ teaspoons ground cinnamon
- ⅔ teaspoon ground cardamom
- ⅔ teaspoon ground nutmeg
- 2¼ teaspoons bread machine yeast

**Directions**
1. **Preparing the Ingredients.**
Choose the size of loaf of your preference and then measure the ingredients.
Add all of the ingredients mentioned previously in the list. Close the lid after placing the pan in the bread machine.
2. **Select the Bake cycle**
Turn on the bread machine. Select the White/Basic setting, select the loaf size, and the crust color. Press start.
When the cycle is finished, carefully remove the pan from the bread maker and let it rest.
Remove the bread from the pan, put in a wire rack to Cool about 10 minutes. Slice


## Fragrant Herb Bread

### PREP: 10 MINUTES /MAKES 1 LOAF

**Ingredients**
- 12 slices bread (1½ pounds)
- 1⅛ cups water, at 80°F to 90°F
- 1½ tablespoons melted butter, cooled
- 1½ tablespoons sugar
- 1 teaspoon salt
- 3 tablespoons skim milk powder
- 1 teaspoon dried thyme
- 1 teaspoon dried chives
- 1 teaspoon dried oregano
- 3 cups white bread flour
- 1¼ teaspoons bread machine or instant yeast

**Directions**

1.  **Preparing the Ingredients.**
Choose the size of loaf of your preference and then measure the ingredients.
Add all of the ingredients mentioned previously in the list. Close the lid after placing the pan in the bread machine.
2.  **Select the Bake cycle**
Turn on the bread machine. Select the White/Basic setting, select the loaf size, and the crust color. Press start.
When the cycle is finished, carefully remove the pan from the bread maker and let it rest.
Remove the bread from the pan, put in a wire rack to Cool about 10 minutes. Slice

# Citrus and Walnut Bread

**PREP: 10 MINUTES PLUS FERMENTING TIME /MAKES 14 SLICES**

## Ingredients
- ¾ cup lemon yogurt
- ½ cup orange juice
- 5 tsp caster sugar
- 1 tsp salt
- 2.5 Tbsp butter
- 2 cups unbleached white bread flour
- 1½ tsp easy blend dried yeast
- ⅓ cup chopped walnuts
- 2 tsp grated lemon rind
- 2 tsp grated orange rind

## Directions
1.  **Preparing the Ingredients.**
Choose the size of loaf of your preference and then measure the ingredients.
Add all of the ingredients mentioned previously in the list, except for the walnuts and orange and lemon rind.
Close the lid after placing the pan in the bread machine.
2.  **Select the Bake cycle**
Close the lid, select the basic bread, medium crust setting on your bread machine, and press start.
Add the walnuts, and orange and lemon rind during the 2nd kneading cycle:
When the bread machine has finished baking, remove the bread and put it on a cooling rack.

# Almond Milk Bread

**PREP: 10 MINUTES /MAKES 1 LOAF**

## Ingredients
- 12 slice bread (1½ pounds)
- ¾ cup lukewarm milk
- 2 eggs, at room temperature
- 2 tablespoons butter, melted and cooled
- ¼ cup sugar
- 1 teaspoon table salt

- 2 teaspoons lemon zest
- 3 cups white bread flour
- 2 teaspoons bread machine yeast
- ⅓ cup slivered almonds, chopped
- ⅓ cup golden raisins, chopped

**Directions**

**1. Preparing the Ingredients.**

Choose the size of loaf of your preference and then measure the ingredients.

Add all of the ingredients mentioned previously in the list, except for the raisins and almonds.

Close the lid after placing the pan in the bread machine.

**2. Select the Bake cycle**

Turn on the bread maker. Select the White/Basic or Fruit/Nut (if your machine has this setting) setting, then the loaf size, and finally the crust color. Start the cycle.

When the machine signals to add ingredients, add the raisins and almonds.

When the cycle is finished, carefully remove the pan from the bread maker and let it rest.

Remove the bread from the pan, put in a wire rack to Cool about 10 minutes. Slice

# Rosemary Bread

**PREP: 10 MINUTES /MAKES 1 LOAF**

**Ingredients**
- 12 slice bread (1½ pounds)
- 1¼ cups water, at 80°F to 90°F
- 2½ tablespoons melted butter, cooled
- 1 tablespoon sugar
- 1½ teaspoons salt
- 1½ tablespoons finely chopped fresh rosemary
- 3 cups white bread flour
- 2 teaspoons bread machine or instant yeast

**Directions**

**1. Preparing the Ingredients.**

Choose the size of loaf of your preference and then measure the ingredients.

Add all of the ingredients mentioned previously in the list.

Close the lid after placing the pan in the bread machine.

**2. Select the Bake cycle**

Turn on the bread machine. Select the White/Basic setting, select the loaf size, and the crust color. Press start.

When the cycle is finished, carefully remove the pan from the bread maker and let it rest.

Remove the bread from the pan, put in a wire rack to Cool about 10 minutes. Slice

# Cinnamon Milk Bread

**PREP: 10 MINUTES /MAKES 1 LOAF**

**Ingredients**
- 12 slice bread (1½ pounds)
- 1 cup lukewarm milk

- 1 egg, at room temperature
- ¼ cup unsalted butter, melted
- ½ cup sugar
- ½ teaspoon table salt
- 3 cups white bread flour
- 1½ teaspoons ground cinnamon
- 2 teaspoons bread machine yeast

**Directions**

**1. Preparing the Ingredients.**

Choose the size of loaf of your preference and then measure the ingredients.

Add all of the ingredients mentioned previously in the list.

Close the lid after placing the pan in the bread machine.

**2. Select the Bake cycle**

Turn on the bread machine. Select the White/Basic setting, select the loaf size, and the crust color. Press start.

When the cycle is finished, carefully remove the pan from the bread maker and let it rest.

Remove the bread from the pan, put in a wire rack to Cool about 10 minutes. Slice

# Spicy Cajun Bread

**PREP: 10 MINUTES /MAKES 1 LOAF**

**Ingredients**

- 12 slice bread (1½ pounds)
- 1⅛ cups water, at 80°F to 90°F
- 1½ tablespoons melted butter, cooled
- 1 tablespoon tomato paste
- 1½ tablespoons sugar
- 1½ teaspoons salt
- 3 tablespoons skim milk powder
- ¾ tablespoon Cajun seasoning
- ¼ teaspoon onion powder
- 3 cups white bread flour
- 1¼ teaspoons bread machine or instant yeast

**Directions**

**1. Preparing the Ingredients.**

Choose the size of loaf of your preference and then measure the ingredients.

Add all of the ingredients mentioned previously in the list.

Close the lid after placing the pan in the bread machine.

**2. Select the Bake cycle**

Turn on the bread machine. Select the White/Basic setting, select the loaf size, and the crust color. Press start.

When the cycle is finished, carefully remove the pan from the bread maker and let it rest.

Remove the bread from the pan, put in a wire rack to Cool about 10 minutes. Slice

# Oat Nut Bread

**PREP: 10 MINUTE S PLUS FERMENTING TIME /MAKES 1 LOAF**

## Ingredients

- 1¼ cups water
- ½ cup quick oats
- ¼ cup brown sugar, firmly packed
- 1 Tbsp butter
- 1½ tsp salt
- 3 cups bread flour
- ¾ cup chopped walnuts
- 1 package dry bread yeast

## Directions

### 1. Preparing the Ingredients

Choose the size of loaf of your preference and then measure the ingredients.

Add all of the ingredients mentioned previously in the list.

Close the lid after placing the pan in the bread machine.

### 2. Select the Bake cycle

Close the lid, select the rapid rise, medium crust setting on your bread machine, and press start.

When the bread machine has finished baking, remove the bread and put it on a cooling rack.

# Hazelnut Honey Bread

**PREP: 10 MINUTES /MAKES 1 LOAF**

## Ingredients

- 16 slices bread (2 pounds)
- 1⅓ cups lukewarm milk
- 2 eggs, at room temperature
- 5 tablespoons unsalted butter, melted
- ¼ cup honey
- 1 teaspoon pure vanilla extract
- 1 teaspoon table salt
- 4 cups white bread flour
- 1 cup toasted hazelnuts, finely ground
- 2 teaspoons bread machine yeast

## Directions

### 1. Preparing the Ingredients.

Choose the size of loaf of your preference and then measure the ingredients.

Add all of the ingredients mentioned previously in the list.

Close the lid after placing the pan in the bread machine.

### 2. Select the Bake cycle

Turn on the bread machine. Select the White/Basic setting, select the loaf size, and the crust color. Press start.

When the cycle is finished, carefully remove the pan from the bread maker and let it rest.

Remove the bread from the pan, put in a wire rack to Cool about 10 minutes. Slice

# Aromatic Lavender Bread

PREP: 10 MINUTES /MAKES 1 LOAF

**Ingredients**
- 16 slices bread (2 pounds)
- 1½ cups milk, at 80°F to 90°F
- 2 tablespoons melted butter, cooled
- 2 tablespoons sugar
- 2 teaspoons salt
- 2 teaspoons chopped fresh lavender flowers
- 1 teaspoon lemon zest
- ½ teaspoon chopped fresh thyme
- 4 cups white bread flour
- 1½ teaspoons bread machine or instant yeast

**Directions**
**1. Preparing the Ingredients.**
Choose the size of loaf of your preference and then measure the ingredients.
Add all of the ingredients mentioned previously in the list.
Close the lid after placing the pan in the bread machine.
**2. Select the Bake cycle**
Turn on the bread machine. Select the White/Basic setting, select the loaf size, and the crust color. Press start.
When the cycle is finished, carefully remove the pan from the bread maker and let it rest.
Remove the bread from the pan, put in a wire rack to Cool about 10 minutes. Slice

# Cardamom Honey Bread

PREP: 10 MINUTES /MAKES 1 LOAF

**Ingredients**
- 16 slices bread (2 pounds)
- 1⅛ cups lukewarm milk
- 1 egg, at room temperature
- 2 teaspoons unsalted butter, melted
- ¼ cup honey
- 1⅓ teaspoons table salt
- 4 cups white bread flour
- 1⅓ teaspoons ground cardamom
- 1⅔ teaspoons bread machine yeast

**Directions**
**1. Preparing the Ingredients.**
Choose the size of loaf of your preference and then measure the ingredients.
Add all of the ingredients mentioned previously in the list.
Close the lid after placing the pan in the bread machine.
**2. Select the Bake cycle**
Turn on the bread machine. Select the White/Basic setting, select the loaf size, and the crust color. Press

start.

When the cycle is finished, carefully remove the pan from the bread maker and let it rest.

Remove the bread from the pan, put in a wire rack to Cool about 10 minutes. Slice

# Cracked Black Pepper Bread

**PREP: 10 MINUTES /MAKES 1 LOAF**

## Ingredients

- 12 slice bread (1½ pounds)
- 1⅛ cups water, at 80°F to 90°F
- 1½ tablespoons melted butter, cooled
- 1½ tablespoons sugar
- 1 teaspoon salt
- 3 tablespoons skim milk powder
- 1½ tablespoons minced chives
- ¾ teaspoon garlic powder
- ¾ teaspoon freshly cracked black pepper
- 3 cups white bread flour
- 1¼ teaspoons bread machine or instant yeast

## Directions

**1. Preparing the Ingredients.**

Choose the size of loaf of your preference and then measure the ingredients.

Add all of the ingredients mentioned previously in the list.

Close the lid after placing the pan in the bread machine.

**2. Select the Bake cycle**

Turn on the bread machine. Select the White/Basic setting, select the loaf size, and the crust color. Press start.

When the cycle is finished, carefully remove the pan from the bread maker and let it rest.

Remove the bread from the pan, put in a wire rack to Cool about 10 minutes. Slice

# Pistachio Cherry Bread

**PREP: 10 MINUTES /MAKES 1 LOAF**

## Ingredients

- 16 slices bread (2 pounds)
- 1⅛ cups lukewarm water
- 1 egg, at room temperature
- ¼ cup butter, softened
- ¼ cup packed dark brown sugar
- 1½ teaspoons table salt
- 3¾ cups white bread flour
- ½ teaspoon ground nutmeg
- Dash allspice

- 2 teaspoons bread machine yeast
- 1 cup dried cherries
- ½ cup unsalted pistachios, chopped

**Directions**

**1. Preparing the Ingredients.**

Choose the size of loaf of your preference and then measure the ingredients.

Add all of the ingredients mentioned previously in the list, except the pistachios and cherries.

Close the lid after placing the pan in the bread machine.

**2. Select the Bake cycle**

Turn on the bread maker. Select the White/Basic or Fruit/Nut (if your machine has this setting) setting, then the loaf size, and finally the crust color. Press start.

When the machine signals to add ingredients, add the pistachios and cherries.

When the cycle is finished and the bread is baked, carefully remove the pan from the machine. Use a potholder as the handle will be very hot. Let rest for a few minutes.

Remove the bread from the pan and allow to cool on a wire rack for at least 10 minutes before slicing.

# Herb and Garlic Cream Cheese Bread

**PREP: 10 MINUTES /MAKES 1 LOAF**

**Ingredients**

- 12 slices bread (1½ pounds)
- ½ cup water, at 80°F to 90°F
- ½ cup herb and garlic cream cheese, at room temperature
- 1 egg, at room temperature
- 2 tablespoons melted butter, cooled
- 3 tablespoons sugar
- 1 teaspoon salt
- 3 cups white bread flour
- 1½ teaspoons bread machine or instant yeast

**Directions**

**1. Preparing the Ingredients.**

Choose the size of loaf of your preference and then measure the ingredients.

Add all of the ingredients mentioned previously in the list.

Close the lid after placing the pan in the bread machine.

**2. Select the Bake cycle**

Turn on the bread machine. Select the White/Basic setting, select the loaf size, and the crust color. Press start.

When the cycle is finished, carefully remove the pan from the bread maker and let it rest.

Remove the bread from the pan, put in a wire rack to Cool about 10 minutes. Slice

# Mix Seed Raisin Bread

**PREP: 10 MINUTES /MAKES 1 LOAF**

**Ingredients**

- 16 slices bread (2 pounds)
- 1½ cups lukewarm milk

- 2 tablespoons unsalted butter, melted
- 2 tablespoons honey
- 1 teaspoon table salt
- 2½ cups white bread flour
- ¼ cup flaxseed
- ¼ cup sesame seeds
- 1½ cups whole-wheat flour
- 2¼ teaspoons bread machine yeast
- ½ cup raisins

## Directions
### 1. Preparing the Ingredients.
Choose the size of loaf of your preference and then measure the ingredients.

Add all of the ingredients mentioned previously in the list.

Close the lid after placing the pan in the bread machine.
### 2. Select the Bake cycle
Turn on the bread machine. Select the White/Basic setting, select the loaf size, and the crust color. Press start.

When the cycle is finished, carefully remove the pan from the bread maker and let it rest.

Remove the bread from the pan, put in a wire rack to Cool about 10 minutes. Slice

# Grain, Seed And Nut Bread
**PREP: 10 MINUTES /MAKES 1 LOAF**

## Ingredients
- ¼ cup water
- 1 egg
- 3 Tbsp honey
- 1½ tsp butter, softened
- 3¼ cups bread flour
- 1 cup milk
- 1 tsp salt
- ¼ tsp baking soda
- 1 tsp ground cinnamon
- 2½ tsp active dry yeast
- ¾ cup dried cranberries
- ½ cup chopped walnuts
- 1 Tbsp white vinegar
- ½ tsp sugar

## Directions
### 1. Preparing the Ingredients.
Choose the size of loaf of your preference and then measure the ingredients.

Add all of the ingredients mentioned previously in the list.

Close the lid after placing the pan in the bread machine.
### 2. Select the Bake cycle
Turn on the bread machine. Select the White/Basic setting, select the loaf size, and the crust color. Press

start.

When the cycle is finished, carefully remove the pan from the bread maker and let it rest.

Remove the bread from the pan, put in a wire rack to Cool about 10 minutes. Slice

# Honey-Spice Egg Bread
**PREP: 10 MINUTES /MAKES 1 LOAF**

## Ingredients
- 12 slices bread (1½ pounds)
- 1 cup milk, at 80°F to 90°F
- 2 eggs, at room temperature
- 1½ tablespoons melted butter, cooled
- 2 tablespoons honey
- 1 teaspoon salt
- 1 teaspoon ground cinnamon
- ½ teaspoon ground cardamom
- ½ teaspoon ground nutmeg
- 3 cups white bread flour
- 2 teaspoons bread machine or instant yeast

## Directions
**1. Preparing the Ingredients.**

Choose the size of loaf of your preference and then measure the ingredients.

Add all of the ingredients mentioned previously in the list.

Close the lid after placing the pan in the bread machine.

**2. Select the Bake cycle**

Turn on the bread machine. Select the White/Basic setting, select the loaf size, and the crust color. Press start.

When the cycle is finished, carefully remove the pan from the bread maker and let it rest.

Remove the bread from the pan, put in a wire rack to Cool about 10 minutes. Slice


# Anise Honey Bread
**PREP: 10 MINUTES /MAKES 1 LOAF**

## Ingredients
- 16 slices bread (2 pounds)
- 1 cup + 1 tablespoon lukewarm water
- 1 egg, at room temperature
- ⅓ cup butter, melted and cooled
- ⅓ cup honey
- ⅔ teaspoon table salt
- 4 cups white bread flour
- 1⅓ teaspoons anise seed
- 1⅓ teaspoons lemon zest
- 2½ teaspoons bread machine yeast

## Directions
**1. Preparing the Ingredients.**

Choose the size of loaf of your preference and then measure the ingredients.

Add all of the ingredients mentioned previously in the list.

Close the lid after placing the pan in the bread machine.

**2. Select the Bake cycle**

Turn on the bread machine. Select the White/Basic setting, select the loaf size, and the crust color. Press start.

When the cycle is finished, carefully remove the pan from the bread maker and let it rest.

Remove the bread from the pan, put in a wire rack to Cool about 10 minutes. Slice

# Cinnamon Bread

### PREP: 10 MINUTES /MAKES 1 LOAF

**Ingredients**

- 12 slices bread (1½ pounds)
- 1 cup milk, at 80°F to 90°F
- 1 egg, at room temperature
- ¼ cup melted butter, cooled
- ½ cup sugar
- ½ teaspoon salt
- 1½ teaspoons ground cinnamon
- 3 cups white bread flour
- 2 teaspoons bread machine or active dry yeast

**Directions**

**1. Preparing the Ingredients.**

Choose the size of loaf of your preference and then measure the ingredients.

Add all of the ingredients mentioned previously in the list.

Close the lid after placing the pan in the bread machine.

**2. Select the Bake cycle**

Turn on the bread machine. Select the White/Basic setting, select the loaf size, and the crust color. Press start.

When the cycle is finished, carefully remove the pan from the bread maker and let it rest.

Remove the bread from the pan, put in a wire rack to Cool about 10 minutes. Slice

# Basic Pecan Bread

### PREP: 10 MINUTES /MAKES 1 LOAF

**Ingredients**

- 16 slices bread (2 pounds)
- 1⅓ cups lukewarm milk
- 2⅔ tablespoons unsalted butter, melted
- 1 egg, at room temperature
- 2⅔ tablespoons sugar
- 1⅓ teaspoons table salt
- 4 cups white bread flour
- 2 teaspoons bread machine yeast
- 1⅓ cups chopped pecans, toasted

**Directions**
**1.    Preparing the Ingredients.**
Choose the size of loaf of your preference and then measure the ingredients.
Add all of the ingredients mentioned previously in the list, except the toasted pecans.
Close the lid after placing the pan in the bread machine.
**2.  Select the Bake cycle**
Select the White/Basic or Fruit/Nut (if your machine has this setting) setting, then the loaf size, and the crust color. Press start.
When the machine signals to add ingredients, add the toasted pecans.
When the cycle is finished, carefully remove the pan from the bread maker and let it rest.
Remove the bread from the pan, put in a wire rack to Cool about 10 minutes. Slice

# Apple Walnut Bread

PREP: 10 MINUTE S PLUS FERMENTING TIME /MAKES 1 LOAF

**Ingredients**
- ¾ cup unsweetened applesauce
- 4 cups apple juice
- 1 tsp salt
- 3 Tbsp butter
- 1 large egg
- 4 cups bread flour
- ¼ cup brown sugar, packed
- 1¼ tsp cinnamon
- ½ tsp baking soda
- 2 tsp active dry yeast
- ½ cup chopped walnuts
- ½ cup chopped dried cranberries

**Directions**
**1.  Preparing the Ingredients**
Add each ingredient to the bread machine in the order and at the temperature recommended by your bread machine manufacturer.
**2.  Select the Bake cycle**
Close the lid, select the basic bread, medium crust setting on your bread machine, and press start.
When the bread machine has finished baking, remove the bread and put it on a cooling rack.

# Simple Garlic Bread

PREP: 10 MINUTES /MAKES 1 LOAF

**Ingredients**
- 12 slices bread (1½ pounds)
- 1 cup milk, at 70°F to 80°F
- 1½ tablespoons melted butter, cooled
- 1 tablespoon sugar
- 1½ teaspoons salt
- 2 teaspoons garlic powder
- 2 teaspoons chopped fresh parsley

- 3 cups white bread flour
- 1¾ teaspoons bread machine or instant yeast

**Directions**
**1.  Preparing the Ingredients.**
Choose the size of loaf of your preference and then measure the ingredients.
Add all of the ingredients mentioned previously in the list.
Close the lid after placing the pan in the bread machine.
**2.  Select the Bake cycle**
Turn on the bread machine. Select the White/Basic setting, select the loaf size, and the crust color. Press start.
When the cycle is finished, carefully remove the pan from the bread maker and let it rest.
Remove the bread from the pan, put in a wire rack to Cool about 10 minutes. Slice

# Herbed Pesto Bread

**PREP: 10 MINUTES /MAKES 1 LOAF**

**Ingredients**

- 12 slices bread (1½ pounds)
- 1 cup water, at 80°F to 90°F
- 2¼ tablespoons melted butter, cooled
- 1½ teaspoons minced garlic
- ¾ tablespoon sugar
- 1 teaspoon salt
- 3 tablespoons chopped fresh parsley
- 1½ tablespoons chopped fresh basil
- ⅓ cup grated Parmesan cheese
- 3 cups white bread flour
- 1¼ teaspoons bread machine or active dry yeast

**Directions**
**1.  Preparing the Ingredients.**
Choose the size of loaf of your preference and then measure the ingredients.
Add all of the ingredients mentioned previously in the list.
Close the lid after placing the pan in the bread machine.
**2.  Select the Bake cycle**
Turn on the bread machine. Select the White/Basic setting, select the loaf size, and the crust color. Press start.
When the cycle is finished, carefully remove the pan from the bread maker and let it rest.
Remove the bread from the pan, put in a wire rack to Cool about 10 minutes. Slice

# Caraway Rye Bread

**PREP: 10 MINUTES /MAKES 1 LOAF**

**Ingredients**
- 12 slice bread (1½ pounds)
- 1⅛ cups water, at 80°F to 90°F

- 1¾ tablespoons melted butter, cooled
- 3 tablespoons dark brown sugar
- 1½ tablespoons dark molasses
- 1⅛ teaspoons salt
- 1½ teaspoons caraway seed
- ¾ cup dark rye flour
- 2 cups white bread flour
- 1⅛ teaspoons bread machine or instant yeast

**Directions**

**1.  Preparing the Ingredients.**

Choose the size of loaf of your preference and then measure the ingredients.

Add all of the ingredients mentioned previously in the list.

Close the lid after placing the pan in the bread machine.

**2.  Select the Bake cycle**

Turn on the bread machine. Select the White/Basic setting, select the loaf size, and the crust color. Press start.

When the cycle is finished, carefully remove the pan from the bread maker and let it rest.

Remove the bread from the pan, put in a wire rack to Cool about 10 minutes. Slice

# Anise Lemon Bread

**PREP: 10 MINUTES /MAKES 1 LOAF**

**Ingredients**

- 12 slice bread (1½ pounds)
- ¾ cup water, at 80°F to 90°F
- 1 egg, at room temperature
- ¼ cup butter, melted and cooled
- ¼ cup honey
- ½ teaspoon salt
- 1 teaspoon anise seed
- 1 teaspoon lemon zest
- 3 cups white bread flour
- 2 teaspoons bread machine or instant yeast

**Directions**

**1.  Preparing the Ingredients.**

Choose the size of loaf of your preference and then measure the ingredients.

Add all of the ingredients mentioned previously in the list.

Close the lid after placing the pan in the bread machine.

**2.  Select the Bake cycle**

Turn on the bread machine. Select the White/Basic setting, select the loaf size, and the crust color. Press start.

When the cycle is finished, carefully remove the pan from the bread maker and let it rest.

Remove the bread from the pan, put in a wire rack to Cool about 10 minutes. Slice

# Fragrant Cardamom Bread

**PREP: 10 MINUTES /MAKES 1 LOAF**

**Ingredients**

- 12 slices bread (1½ pounds)
- ¾ cup milk, at 80°F to 90°F
- 1 egg, at room temperature
- 1½ teaspoons melted butter, cooled
- 3 tablespoons honey
- 1 teaspoon salt
- 1 teaspoon ground cardamom
- 3 cups white bread flour
- 1¼ teaspoons bread machine or instant yeast

**Directions**

**1. Preparing the Ingredients.**

Choose the size of loaf of your preference and then measure the ingredients.

Add all of the ingredients mentioned previously in the list.

Close the lid after placing the pan in the bread machine.

**2. Select the Bake cycle**

Turn on the bread machine. Select the White/Basic setting, select the loaf size, and the crust color. Press start.

When the cycle is finished, carefully remove the pan from the bread maker and let it rest.

Remove the bread from the pan, put in a wire rack to Cool about 10 minutes. Slice

# Chocolate Mint Bread

**PREP: 10 MINUTES /MAKES 1 LOAF**

**Ingredients**

- 12 slices bread (1½ pounds)
- 1 cup milk, at 80°F to 90°F
- ⅛ teaspoon mint extract
- 1½ tablespoons butter, melted and cooled
- ¼ cup sugar
- 1 teaspoon salt
- 1½ tablespoons unsweetened cocoa powder
- 3 cups white bread flour
- 1¾ teaspoons bread machine or instant yeast
- ½ cup semisweet chocolate chips

**Directions**

**1. Preparing the Ingredients.**

Choose the size of loaf of your preference and then measure the ingredients.

Add all of the ingredients mentioned previously in the list.

Close the lid after placing the pan in the bread machine.

**2. Select the Bake cycle**

Turn on the bread machine. Select the White/Basic setting, select the loaf size, and the crust color. Press start.

When the cycle is finished, carefully remove the pan from the bread maker and let it rest.

Remove the bread from the pan, put in a wire rack to Cool about 5 minutes. Slice

# Molasses Candied-Ginger Bread

**PREP: 10 MINUTES /MAKES 1 LOAF**

**Ingredients**
- 12 slices bread (1½ pounds)
- 1 cup milk, at 80°F to 90°F
- 1 egg, at room temperature
- ¼ cup dark molasses
- 3 tablespoons butter, melted and cooled
- ½ teaspoon salt
- ¼ cup chopped candied ginger
- ½ cup quick oats
- 3 cups white bread flour
- 2 teaspoons bread machine or instant yeast

**Directions**
**1. Preparing the Ingredients.**
Choose the size of loaf of your preference and then measure the ingredients.
Add all of the ingredients mentioned previously in the list.
Close the lid after placing the pan in the bread machine.
**2. Select the Bake cycle**
Turn on the bread machine. Select the White/Basic setting, select the loaf size, and the crust color. Press start.
When the cycle is finished, carefully remove the pan from the bread maker and let it rest.
Remove the bread from the pan, put in a wire rack to Cool about 5 minutes. Slice

# Whole-Wheat Seed Bread

**PREP: 10 MINUTES /MAKES 1 LOAF**

**Ingredients**
- 12 slice bread (1½ pounds)
- 1⅛ cups water, at 80°F to 90°F
- 1½ tablespoons honey
- 1½ tablespoons melted butter, cooled
- ¾ teaspoon salt
- 2½ cups whole-wheat flour
- ¾ cup white bread flour
- 3 tablespoons raw sunflower seeds
- 1 tablespoon sesame seeds
- 1½ teaspoons bread machine or instant yeast

**Directions**
**1. Preparing the Ingredients.**
Choose the size of loaf of your preference and then measure the ingredients.
Add all of the ingredients mentioned previously in the list.
Close the lid after placing the pan in the bread machine.
**2. Select the Bake cycle**

Turn on the bread machine. Select the Whole-Wheat/Whole-Grain bread, select the loaf size, and select light or medium crust. Press start.

When the cycle is finished, carefully remove the pan from the bread maker and let it rest.

Remove the bread from the pan, put in a wire rack to Cool about 5 minutes. Slice

# Multigrain Bread

**PREP: 10 MINUTES /MAKES 1 LOAF**

## Ingredients

- 12 slice bread (1½ pounds)
- 1 cup plus 2 tablespoons water, at 80°F to 90°F
- 2 tablespoons melted butter, cooled
- 1½ tablespoons honey
- 1½ teaspoons salt
- 1 cup plus 2 tablespoons multigrain flour
- 2 cups white bread flour
- 1½ teaspoons bread machine or active dry yeast

## Directions

### 1. Preparing the Ingredients.

Choose the size of loaf of your preference and then measure the ingredients.

Add all of the ingredients mentioned previously in the list.

Close the lid after placing the pan in the bread machine.

### 2. Select the Bake cycle

Turn on the bread machine. Select the White/Basic setting, select the loaf size, and the crust color. Press start.

When the cycle is finished, carefully remove the pan from the bread maker and let it rest.

Remove the bread from the pan, put in a wire rack to Cool about 5 minutes. Slice

# Pecan Raisin Bread

**PREP: 10 MINUTE S PLUS FERMENTING TIME /MAKES 1 LOAF**

## Ingredients

1 cup plus 2 Tbsp water (70°F to 80°F)

8 tsp butter

1 egg

6 Tbsp sugar

¼ cup nonfat dry milk powder

1 tsp salt

4 cups bread flour

1 Tbsp active dry yeast

1 cup finely chopped pecans

1 cup raisins

## Directions

### 1. Preparing the Ingredients

Add each ingredient to the bread machine except the pecans and raisins in the order and at the temperature recommended by your bread machine manufacturer.

### 2. Select the Bake cycle

Close the lid, select the basic bread, medium crust setting on your bread machine, and press start.
Just before the final kneading, add the pecans and raisins.
When the bread machine has finished baking, remove the bread and put it on a cooling rack.

# Toasted Pecan Bread

**PREP: 10 MINUTES /MAKES 1 LOAF**

**Ingredients**
- 12 slice bread (1½ pounds)
- 1 cup milk, at 70°F to 80°F
- 2 tablespoons melted butter, cooled
- 1 egg, at room temperature
- 2 tablespoons sugar
- 1 teaspoon salt
- 3 cups white bread flour
- 1½ teaspoons bread machine or instant yeast
- 1 cup chopped pecans, toasted

**Directions**
**1. Preparing the Ingredients.**
Add each ingredient to the bread machine except the pecans and raisins in the order and at the temperature recommended by your bread machine manufacturer.
**2. Select the Bake cycle**
Program the machine for Basic/White bread, select light or medium crust, and press Start.
When the machine signals, add the pecans, or put them in a nut/raisin hopper and the machine will add them automatically
When the cycle is finished, carefully remove the pan from the bread maker and let it rest.
Remove the bread from the pan, put in a wire rack to Cool about 5 minutes. Slice

# Quinoa Oatmeal Bread

**PREP: 10 MINUTES /MAKES 1 LOAF**

**Ingredients**
- ⅓ cup uncooked quinoa
- ⅔ cup water (for cooking quinoa)
- 1 cup buttermilk
- 1 tsp salt
- 1 Tbsp sugar
- 1 Tbsp honey
- 4 Tbsp unsalted butter
- ½ cup quick-cooking oats
- ½ cup whole wheat flour
- 1½ cups bread flour

**Directions**
**1. Preparing the Ingredients**
Add quinoa to a saucepan. Cover it with water. Bring to boil. Cook for 5 minutes, covered. Turn off and

leave the quinoa covered for 10 minutes. Add each ingredient to the bread machine in the order and at the temperature recommended by your bread machine manufacturer.

**2. Select the Bake cycle**

Close the lid, select the whole grain, medium crust setting on your bread machine and press start. When the bread machine has finished baking, remove the bread and put it on a cooling rack.

# Market Seed Bread

PREP: 10 MINUTES /MAKES 1 LOAF

**Ingredients**
- 12 slice bread (1½ pounds)
- 1 cup plus 2 tablespoons milk, at 80°F to 90°F
- 1½ tablespoons melted butter, cooled
- 1½ tablespoons honey
- ¾ teaspoon salt
- 3 tablespoons flaxseed
- 3 tablespoons sesame seeds
- 1½ tablespoons poppy seeds
- 1¼ cups whole-wheat flour
- 1¾ cups white bread flour
- 1¾ teaspoons bread machine or instant yeast

**Directions**

**1. Preparing the Ingredients.**

Choose the size of loaf of your preference and then measure the ingredients.

Add all of the ingredients mentioned previously in the list.

Close the lid after placing the pan in the bread machine.

**2. Select the Bake cycle**

Turn on the bread machine. Select the White/Basic setting, select the loaf size, and the crust color. Press start.

When the cycle is finished, carefully remove the pan from the bread maker and let it rest.

Remove the bread from the pan, put in a wire rack to Cool about 5 minutes. Slice

# Pesto Nut Bread

PREP: 10 MINUTES /MAKES 14 SLICES

**Ingredients**
- 1 cup plus 2 Tbsp water
- 3 cups Gold Medal Better for Bread flour
- 2 Tbsp sugar
- 1 tsp salt
- 1¼ tsp bread machine or quick active dry yeast
- For the pesto filling:
- ⅓ cup basil pesto
- 2 Tbsp Gold Medal Better for Bread flour
- ⅓ cup pine nuts

**Directions**

**1. Preparing the Ingredients**

Add each ingredient to the bread machine in the order and at the temperature recommended by your bread machine manufacturer.

**2. Select the Bake cycle**

Close the lid, select the basic bread, medium crust setting on your bread machine, and press start.

In a small bowl, combine pesto and 2 Tbsp of flour until well blended. Stir in the pine nuts. Add the filling 5 minutes before the last kneading cycle ends.

When the bread machine has finished baking, remove the bread and put it on a cooling rack.

# Cracked Wheat Bread

**PREP: 10 MINUTES /MAKES 1 LOAF**

**Ingredients**
- 12 slice bread (1½ pounds)
- ¼ cup cracked wheat
- 1¼ cups boiling water
- ¼ cup melted butter, cooled
- 3 tablespoons honey
- 1½ teaspoons salt
- 1 cup whole-wheat flour
- 2 cups white bread flour
- 2 teaspoons bread machine or instant yeast

**Directions**

**1. Preparing the Ingredients.**

Place the cracked wheat and water in the bucket of your bread machine for 30 minutes or until the liquid is 80°F to 90°F.

Place the remaining ingredients in your bread machine as recommended by the manufacturer.

**2. Select the Bake cycle**

Turn on the bread machine. Select the White/Basic setting, select the loaf size, and the crust color. Press start.

When the cycle is finished, carefully remove the pan from the bread maker and let it rest.

Remove the bread from the pan, put in a wire rack to Cool about 5 minutes. Slice

# Double Coconut Bread

**PREP: 10 MINUTES /MAKES 1 LOAF**

**Ingredients**
- 12 slice bread (1½ pounds)
- 1 cup milk, at 80°F to 90°F
- 1 egg, at room temperature
- 1½ tablespoons melted butter, cooled
- 2 teaspoons pure coconut extract
- 2½ tablespoons sugar
- ¾ teaspoon salt
- ½ cup sweetened shredded coconut
- 3 cups white bread flour
- 1½ teaspoons bread machine or instant yeast

**Directions**

**1. Preparing the Ingredients.**

Choose the size of loaf of your preference and then measure the ingredients.

Add all of the ingredients mentioned previously in the list.

Close the lid after placing the pan in the bread machine.

**2. Select the Bake cycle**

Program the machine for Sweet bread, select light or medium crust, and press Start.

When the cycle is finished, carefully remove the pan from the bread maker and let it rest.

Remove the bread from the pan, put in a wire rack to Cool about 5 minutes. Slice

# Seed Bread

**PREP: 10 MINUTES /MAKES 1 LOAF**

**Ingredients**

- 3 Tbsp flax seed
- 1 Tbsp sesame seeds
- 1 Tbsp poppy seeds
- ¾ cup water
- 1 Tbsp honey
- 1 Tbsp canola oil
- ½ tsp salt
- 1½ cups bread flour
- 5 Tbsp wholemeal flour
- 1¼ tsp dried active baking yeast

**Directions**

**1. Preparing the Ingredients**

Add each ingredient to the bread machine in the order and at the temperature recommended by your bread machine manufacturer.

**2. Select the Bake cycle**

Close the lid, select the basic bread, medium crust setting on your bread machine, and press start.

When the bread machine has finished baking, remove the bread and put it on a cooling rack.

# Honeyed Bulgur Bread

**PREP: 10 MINUTES /MAKES 1 LOAF**

**Ingredients**

- 12 slice bread (1½ pounds)
- ¾ cup boiling water
- 3 tablespoons bulgur wheat
- 3 tablespoons quick oats
- 2 eggs, at room temperature
- 1½ tablespoons melted butter, cooled
- 2¼ tablespoons honey
- 1 teaspoon salt
- 2¼ cups white bread flour
- 1½ teaspoons bread machine or instant yeast

**Directions**

**1. Preparing the Ingredients.**

Place the water, bulgur, and oats in the bucket of your bread machine for 30 minutes or until the liquid is 80°F to 90°F.

Place the remaining ingredients in your bread machine as recommended by the manufacturer.

**2. Select the Bake cycle**

Turn on the bread machine. Select the White/Basic setting, select the loaf size, and the crust color. Press start.

When the cycle is finished, carefully remove the pan from the bread maker and let it rest.

Remove the bread from the pan, put in a wire rack to Cool about 5 minutes. Slice

# Chia Seed Bread

**PREP: 10 MINUTES /MAKES 14 SLICES**

**Ingredients**

- ¼ cup chia seeds
- ¾ cup hot water
- 2⅜ cups water
- ¼ cup oil
- ½ lemon, zest and juice
- 1¾ cups white flour
- 1¾ cups whole wheat flour
- 2 tsp baking powder
- 1 tsp salt
- 1 Tbsp sugar
- 2½ tsp quick rise yeast

**Directions**

**1. Preparing the Ingredients**

Add the chia seeds to a bowl, cover with hot water, mix well and let them stand until they are soaked and gelatinous, and don't feel warm to touch.

Add each ingredient to the bread machine in the order and at the temperature recommended by your bread machine manufacturer.

**2. Select the Bake cycle**

Close the lid, select the basic bread, medium crust setting on your bread machine, and press start.

When the mixing blade stops moving, open the machine and mix everything by hand with a spatula.

When the bread machine has finished baking, remove the bread and put it on a cooling rack.

# Flaxseed Honey Bread

**PREP: 10 MINUTES /MAKES 1 LOAF**

**Ingredients**

- 12 slices bread (1½ pounds)
- 1⅛ cups milk, at 80°F to 90°F
- 1½ tablespoons melted butter, cooled
- 1½ tablespoons honey
- 1 teaspoon salt
- ¼ cup flaxseed
- 3 cups white bread flour

- 1¼ teaspoons bread machine or instant yeast

**Directions**

**1. Preparing the Ingredients .**

Choose the size of loaf of your preference and then measure the ingredients.

Add all of the ingredients mentioned previously in the list.

Close the lid after placing the pan in the bread machine.

**2. Select the Bake cycle .**

Turn on the bread machine. Select the White/Basic setting, select the loaf size, and the crust color. Press start.

When the cycle is finished, carefully remove the pan from the bread maker and let it rest.

Remove the bread from the pan, put in a wire rack to Cool about 5 minutes. Slice

# Chia Sesame Bread

**PREP: 10 MINUTES /MAKES 1 LOAF**

**Ingredients**

- 12 slice bread (1½ pounds)
- 1 cup plus 2 tablespoons water, at 80°F to 90°F
- 1½ tablespoons melted butter, cooled
- 1½ tablespoons sugar
- 1⅛ teaspoons salt
- ½ cup ground chia seeds
- 1½ tablespoons sesame seeds
- 2½ cups white bread flour
- 1½ teaspoons bread machine or instant yeast

**Directions**

**1. Preparing the Ingredients.**

Choose the size of loaf of your preference and then measure the ingredients.

Add all of the ingredients mentioned previously in the list.

Close the lid after placing the pan in the bread machine.

**2. Select the Bake cycle**

Turn on the bread machine. Select the White/Basic setting, select the loaf size, and the crust color. Press start.

When the cycle is finished, carefully remove the pan from the bread maker and let it rest.

Remove the bread from the pan, put in a wire rack to Cool about 5 minutes. Slice

# Sesame French Bread

**PREP: 10 MINUTES /MAKES 1 LOAF**

**Ingredients**

- ⅞ cup water
- 1 Tbsp butter, softened
- 3 cups bread flour
- 2 tsp sugar
- 1 tsp salt
- 2 tsp yeast

- 2 Tbsp sesame seeds toasted

**Directions**

**1.  Preparing the Ingredients**

Add each ingredient to the bread machine in the order and at the temperature recommended by your bread machine manufacturer.

**2.  Select the Bake cycle**

Close the lid, select the French bread, medium crust setting on your bread machine and press start. When the bread machine has finished baking, remove the bread and put it on a cooling rack.

# Quinoa Whole-Wheat Bread

**PREP: 10 MINUTES /MAKES 1 LOAF**

**Ingredients**

- 12 slice bread (1½ pounds)
- 1 cup milk, at 80°F to 90°F
- ⅔ cup cooked quinoa, cooled
- ¼ cup melted butter, cooled
- 1 tablespoon sugar
- 1 teaspoon salt
- ¼ cup quick oats
- ¾ cup whole-wheat flour
- 1½ cups white bread flour
- 1½ teaspoons bread machine or instant yeast

**Directions**

**1.  Preparing the Ingredients.**

Choose the size of loaf of your preference and then measure the ingredients.

Add all of the ingredients mentioned previously in the list.

Close the lid after placing the pan in the bread machine.

**2.  Select the Bake cycle**

Turn on the bread machine. Select the White/Basic setting, select the loaf size, and the crust color. Press start.

When the cycle is finished, carefully remove the pan from the bread maker and let it rest.

Remove the bread from the pan, put in a wire rack to Cool about 5 minutes. Slice

# Peanut Butter Bread

**PREP: 10 MINUTES /MAKES 1 LOAF**

**Ingredients**

- 1 cup peanut butter
- 1 cup milk, at 70°F to 80°F
- ½ cup packed light brown sugar
- ¼ cup sugar
- ¼ cup (½ stick) butter, at room temperature
- 1 egg, at room temperature
- 2 teaspoons pure vanilla extract

- 2 cups all-purpose flour
- 1 tablespoon baking powder
- ½ teaspoon salt

**Directions**

**1. Preparing the Ingredients.**

Place the peanut butter, milk, brown sugar, sugar, butter, egg, and vanilla in your bread machine.

**2. Select the Bake cycle**

Program the machine for Quick/Rapid bread and press Start.

While the wet ingredients are mixing, stir together the flour, baking powder, and salt in a small bowl.

After the first fast mixing is done and the machine signals, add the dry ingredients.

When the cycle is finished, carefully remove the pan from the bread maker and let it rest.

Remove the bread from the pan, put in a wire rack to Cool about 5 minutes. Slice

# Toasted Hazelnut Bread

**PREP: 10 MINUTES /MAKES 1 LOAF**

**Ingredients**

- 12 slice bread (1½ pounds)
- 1 cup milk, at 70°F to 80°F
- 1 egg, at room temperature
- 3¾ tablespoons melted butter, cooled
- 3 tablespoons honey
- ¾ teaspoon pure vanilla extract
- ¾ teaspoon salt
- ¾ cup finely ground toasted hazelnuts
- 3 cups white bread flour
- 1½ teaspoons bread machine or instant yeast

**Directions**

**1. Preparing the Ingredients.**

Choose the size of loaf of your preference and then measure the ingredients.

Add all of the ingredients mentioned previously in the list.

Close the lid after placing the pan in the bread machine.

**2. Select the Bake cycle**

Turn on the bread machine. Select the White/Basic setting, select the loaf size, and the crust color. Press start.

When the cycle is finished, carefully remove the pan from the bread maker and let it rest.

Remove the bread from the pan, put in a wire rack to Cool about 5 minutes. Slice

# Oatmeal Seed Bread

**PREP: 10 MINUTES /MAKES 1 LOAF**

**Ingredients**

- 12 slice bread (1½ pounds)
- 1⅛ cups water, at 80°F to 90°F
- 3 tablespoons melted butter, cooled
- 3 tablespoons light brown sugar

- 1½ teaspoons salt
- 3 tablespoons raw sunflower seeds
- 3 tablespoons pumpkin seeds
- 2 tablespoons sesame seeds
- 1 teaspoon anise seeds
- 1 cup quick oats
- 2¼ cups white bread flour
- 1½ teaspoons bread machine or instant yeast

**Directions**

**1. Preparing the Ingredients.**

Choose the size of loaf of your preference and then measure the ingredients.

Add all of the ingredients mentioned previously in the list.

Close the lid after placing the pan in the bread machine.

**2. Select the Bake cycle**

Turn on the bread machine. Select the White/Basic setting, select the loaf size, and the crust color. Press start.

When the cycle is finished, carefully remove the pan from the bread maker and let it rest.

Remove the bread from the pan, put in a wire rack to Cool about 5 minutes. Slice

# Nutty Wheat Bread

**PREP: 10 MINUTES /MAKES 1 LOAF**

**Ingredients**
- 12 slice bread (1½ pounds)
- 1½ cups water, at 80°F to 90°F
- 2 tablespoons melted butter, cooled
- 1 tablespoon sugar
- 1½ teaspoons salt
- 1¼ cups whole-wheat flour
- 2 cups white bread flour
- 1¼ teaspoons bread machine or instant yeast
- 2 tablespoons chopped almonds
- 2 tablespoons chopped pecans
- 2 tablespoons sunflower seeds

**Directions**

**1. Preparing the Ingredients.**

Place the ingredients, except the almonds, pecans, and seeds, in your bread machine as recommended by the manufacturer.

**2. Select the Bake cycle**

Turn on the bread machine. Select the White/Basic setting, select the loaf size, and the crust color. Press start.

When the cycle is finished, carefully remove the pan from the bread maker and let it rest.

Remove the bread from the pan, put in a wire rack to Cool about 5 minutes. Slice

# Sunflower Bread

## Ingredients

- 12 slice bread (1½ pounds)
- 1 cup water, at 80°F to 90°F
- 1 egg, at room temperature
- 3 tablespoons melted butter, cooled
- 3 tablespoons skim milk powder
- 1½ tablespoons honey
- 1½ teaspoons salt
- ¾ cup raw sunflower seeds
- 3 cups white bread flour
- 1 teaspoon bread machine or instant yeast

## Directions

### 1. Preparing the Ingredients.

Choose the size of loaf of your preference and then measure the ingredients.

Add all of the ingredients mentioned previously in the list.

Close the lid after placing the pan in the bread machine.

### 2. Select the Bake cycle

Turn on the bread machine. Select the White/Basic setting, select the loaf size, and the crust color. Press start.

When the cycle is finished, carefully remove the pan from the bread maker and let it rest.

Remove the bread from the pan, put in a wire rack to Cool about 5 minutes. Slice

# Raisin Seed Bread

**PREP: 10 MINUTES /MAKES 1 LOAF**

## Ingredients

- 12 slice bread (1½ pounds)
- 1 cup plus 2 tablespoons milk, at 80°F to 90°F
- 1½ tablespoons melted butter, cooled
- 1½ tablespoons honey
- ¾ teaspoon salt
- 3 tablespoons flaxseed
- 3 tablespoons sesame seeds
- 1¼ cups whole-wheat flour
- 1¾ cups white bread flour
- 1¾ teaspoons bread machine or instant yeast
- ⅓ cup raisins

## Directions

### 1. Preparing the Ingredients.

Choose the size of loaf of your preference and then measure the ingredients.

Add all of the ingredients mentioned previously in the list except the raisins.

Close the lid after placing the pan in the bread machine.

### 2. Select the Bake cycle

Program the machine for Basic/White bread, select light or medium crust, and press Start.

Add the raisins when the bread machine signals, or place the raisins in the raisin/nut hopper and let the machine add them.

When the cycle is finished, carefully remove the pan from the bread maker and let it rest.

Remove the bread from the pan, put in a wire rack to Cool about 5 minutes. Slice

# Rosemary Bread

**PREP: 10 MINUTES /MAKES 14 SLICES**

## Ingredients

- 1⅓ cups milk
- 4 Tbsp butter
- 3 cups bread flour
- 1 cup one minute oatmeal
- 1 tsp salt
- 6 tsp white granulated sugar
- 1 Tbsp onion powder
- 1 Tbsp dried rosemary
- 1½ tsp bread machine yeast

## Directions

**1. Preparing the Ingredients**

Add each ingredient to the bread machine in the order and at the temperature recommended by your bread machine manufacturer.

**2. Select the Bake cycle**

Close the lid, select the basic bread, medium crust setting on your bread machine and press start.

After the bread machine has finished kneading, sprinkle some rosemary on top of the bread dough.

When the bread machine has finished baking, remove the bread and put it on a cooling rack.

# Cajun Bread

**PREP: 10 MINUTES /MAKES 14 SLICES**

## Ingredients

- ½ cup water
- ¼ cup chopped onion
- ¼ cup chopped green bell pepper
- 2 tsp finely chopped garlic
- 2 tsp soft butter
- 2 cups bread flour
- 1 Tbsp sugar
- 1 tsp Cajun
- ½ tsp salt
- 1 tsp active dry yeast

## Directions

**1. Preparing the Ingredients**

Add each ingredient to the bread machine in the order and at the temperature recommended by your bread machine manufacturer.

**2. Select the Bake cycle**

Close the lid, select the basic bread, medium crust setting on your bread machine and press start.

When the bread machine has finished baking, remove the bread and put it on a cooling rack.

# Turmeric Bread

**PREP: 10 MINUTES /MAKES 14 SLICES**

## Ingredients
- 1 tsp dried yeast
- 4 cups strong white flour
- 1 tsp turmeric powder
- 2 tsp beetroot powder
- 2 Tbsp olive oil
- 1.5 tsp salt
- 1 tsp chili flakes
- 1⅜ water

## Directions
**1.  Preparing the Ingredients**
Add each ingredient to the bread machine in the order and at the temperature recommended by your bread machine manufacturer.
**2.  Select the Bake cycle**
Close the lid, select the basic bread, medium crust setting on your bread machine and press start.
When the bread machine has finished baking, remove the bread and put it on a cooling rack.

# Rosemary Bread

**PREP: 10 MINUTES /MAKES 12 SLICES**

## Ingredients
- 1 cup warm water, about 105°F
- 2 tablespoons butter, softened
- 1 egg
- 3 cups all-purpose flour
- 1/4 cup whole wheat flour
- 1/3 cup sugar
- 1 teaspoon salt
- 3 teaspoons bread maker yeast
- 2 tablespoons rosemary, freshly chopped
- For the topping:
- 1 egg, room temperature
- 1 teaspoon milk, room temperature
- Garlic powder
- Sea salt

## Directions
**1.  Preparing the Ingredients**
Place all of the ingredients in the bread maker pan in the order listed above.
**2.  Select the Bake cycle**
Select Dough cycle.
When dough is kneaded, place on parchment paper on a flat surface and roll into two loaves; set aside and allow to rise for 30 minutes. Preheat a pizza stone in an oven on 375°F for 30 minutes. For the

topping, add the egg and milk to a small mixing bowl and whisk to create an egg wash. Baste the formed loaves and sprinkle evenly with garlic powder and sea salt. Allow to rise for 40 minutes, lightly covered, in a warm area. Bake for 15 to 18 minutes or until golden brown. Serve warm.

# Pumpkin Coconut Almond Bread

**PREP: 5 MINUTES /MAKES 12 SLICES**

**Ingredients**
- 1/3 cup vegetable oil
- 3 large eggs
- 1 1/2 cups canned pumpkin puree
- 1 cup sugar
- 1 1/2 teaspoons baking powder
- 1/2 teaspoon baking soda
- 1/4 teaspoon salt
- 1 tablespoon allspice
- 3 cups all-purpose flour
- 1/2 cup coconut flakes, plus a small handful for the topping
- 2/3 cup slivered almonds, plus a tablespoonful for the topping
- Non-stick cooking spray

**Directions**

**1. Preparing the Ingredients**

Spray bread maker pan with non-stick cooking spray. Mix oil, eggs, and pumpkin in a large mixing bowl.

Mix remaining ingredients together in a separate mixing bowl. Add wet ingredients to bread maker pan, and dry ingredients on top.

**2. Select the Bake cycle**

Select Dough cycle and press Start. Open lid and sprinkle top of bread with reserved coconut and almonds.

Set to Rapid for 1 hour 30 minutes and bake. Cool for 10 minutes on a wire rack before serving.

# Gluten-Free Oat & Honey Bread

**PREP: 5 MINUTES /MAKES 12 SLICES**

**Ingredients**
- 1 1/4 cups warm water
- 3 tablespoons honey
- 2 eggs
- 3 tablespoons butter, melted
- 1 1/4 cups gluten-free oats
- 1 1/4 cups brown rice flour
- 1/2 cup potato starch
- 2 teaspoons xanthan gum
- 1 1/2 teaspoons sugar
- 3/4 teaspoon salt
- 1 1/2 tablespoons active dry yeast

**Directions**

1. **Preparing the Ingredients**

Add ingredients in the order listed above, except for yeast.

Make a well in the center of the dry ingredients and add the yeast.

2. **Select the Bake cycle**

Select Gluten-Free cycle, light crust color, and press Start.

Remove bread and allow the bread to cool on its side on a cooling rack for 20 minutes before slicing to serve.

# VEGETABLE BREAD

## Beetroot Bread

**PREP: 10 MINUTES /MAKES 1 LOAF**

**Ingredients**

- 16 slice bread (1½ pounds)
- 1 cup lukewarm water
- 1 cup grated raw beetroot
- 2 tablespoons unsalted butter, melted
- 2 tablespoons sugar
- 2 teaspoons table salt
- 4 cups white bread flour
- 1⅔ teaspoons bread machine yeast

**Directions**

1. **Preparing the Ingredients.**

Choose the size of loaf of your preference and then measure the ingredients.

Add all of the ingredients mentioned previously in the list.

Close the lid after placing the pan in the bread machine.

2. **Select the Bake cycle**

Turn on the bread machine. Select the White/Basic setting, select the loaf size, and the crust color. Press start.

When the cycle is finished, carefully remove the pan from the bread maker and let it rest.

Remove the bread from the pan, put in a wire rack to Cool about 5 minutes. Slice

## Yeasted Carrot Bread

**PREP: 10 MINUTES /MAKES 1 LOAF**

**Ingredients**

- 12 slice bread (1½ pounds)
- ¾ cup milk, at 80°F to 90°F
- 3 tablespoons melted butter, cooled
- 1 tablespoon honey
- 1½ cups shredded carrot
- ¾ teaspoon ground nutmeg
- ½ teaspoon salt
- 3 cups white bread flour
- 2¼ teaspoons bread machine or active dry yeast

**Directions**

**1. Preparing the Ingredients.**
Choose the size of loaf of your preference and then measure the ingredients.
Add all of the ingredients mentioned previously in the list.
Close the lid after placing the pan in the bread machine.
**2. Select the Bake cycle**
Turn on the bread machine. Select the Quick/Rapid setting, select the loaf size, and the crust color. Press start.
When the cycle is finished, carefully remove the pan from the bread maker and let it rest.
Remove the bread from the pan, put in a wire rack to Cool about 5 minutes. Slice

# Sweet Potato Bread

**PREP: 10 MINUTES /MAKES 1 LOAF**

## Ingredients

- 12 slice bread (1½ pounds)
- ⅓ cup + 2 tablespoons lukewarm water
- ¾ cup plain sweet potatoes, peeled and mashed
- 1½ tablespoons unsalted butter, melted
- ¼ cup dark brown sugar
- 1 teaspoon table salt
- 3 cups bread flour
- ⅛ teaspoon ground nutmeg
- ⅛ teaspoon cinnamon
- ¾ teaspoon vanilla extract
- 1½ tablespoons dry milk powder
- 1½ teaspoons bread machine yeast

## Directions

**1. Preparing the Ingredients.**
Choose the size of loaf of your preference and then measure the ingredients.
Add all of the ingredients mentioned previously in the list.
Close the lid after placing the pan in the bread machine.
**2. Select the Bake cycle**
Turn on the bread machine. Select the Quick/Rapid setting, select the loaf size, and the crust color. Press start.
When the cycle is finished, carefully remove the pan from the bread maker and let it rest.
Remove the bread from the pan, put in a wire rack to Cool about 5 minutes. Slice

# Sauerkraut Rye Bread

**PREP: 10 MINUTES /MAKES 1 LOAF**

## Ingredients

- 12 slice bread (1½ pounds)
- 1 cup water, at 80°F to 90°F
- 1½ tablespoons melted butter, cooled
- ⅓ cup molasses
- ½ cup drained sauerkraut

- ⅓ teaspoon salt
- 1½ tablespoons unsweetened cocoa powder
- Pinch ground nutmeg
- ¾ cup rye flour
- 2 cups white bread flour
- 1⅔ teaspoons bread machine or instant yeast

**Directions**

**1. Preparing the Ingredients.**

Choose the size of loaf of your preference and then measure the ingredients.

Add all of the ingredients mentioned previously in the list.

Close the lid after placing the pan in the bread machine.

**2. Select the Bake cycle**

Turn on the bread machine. Select the White/Basic setting, select the loaf size, and the crust color. Press start.

When the cycle is finished, carefully remove the pan from the bread maker and let it rest.

Remove the bread from the pan, put in a wire rack to Cool about 5 minutes. Slice

# Garden Vegetable Bread

**PREP: 10 MINUTES /MAKES 14 SLICES**

**Ingredients**

- ½ cup warm buttermilk (70°F to 80°F)
- 3 Tbsp water (70°F to 80°F)
- 1 Tbsp canola oil
- ⅔ cup shredded zucchini
- ¼ cup chopped red sweet pepper
- 2 Tbsp chopped green onions
- 2 Tbsp grated parmesan cheese
- 2 Tbsp sugar
- 1 tsp salt
- ½ tsp lemon-pepper seasoning
- ½ cup old-fashioned oats
- 2½ cup bread flour
- 1½ tsp active dry yeast
- Peppercorns

**Directions**

**1. Preparing the Ingredients.**

Add each ingredient to the bread machine in the order and at the temperature recommended by your bread machine manufacturer.

**2. Select the Bake cycle**

Close the lid, select the basic bread, medium crust setting on your bread machine and press start.

When the bread machine has finished baking, remove the bread and put it on a cooling rack.

# Carrot Coriander Bread

**PREP: 10 MINUTES /MAKES 14 SLICES**

**Ingredients**

- 2-3 freshly grated carrots,
- 1⅛ cup lukewarm water
- 2 Tbsp sunflower oil
- 4 tsp freshly chopped coriander
- 2½ cups unbleached white bread flour
- 2 tsp ground coriander
- 1 tsp salt
- 5 tsp sugar
- 4 tsp easy blend dried yeast

**Directions**

**1.  Preparing the Ingredients.**

Add each ingredient to the bread machine in the order and at the temperature recommended by your bread machine manufacturer.

**2.  Select the Bake cycle**

Close the lid, select the basic bread, medium crust setting on your bread machine, and press start.
When the bread machine has finished baking, remove the bread and put it on a cooling rack.

# Basil Tomato Bread

**PREP: 10 MINUTES /MAKES 1 LOAF**

**Ingredients**

- 12 slice bread (1½ pounds)
- ¾ cup lukewarm tomato sauce
- ¾ tablespoon olive oil
- ¾ tablespoon sugar
- ¾ teaspoon table salt
- 2¼ cups white bread flour
- 1½ tablespoons dried basil
- ¾ tablespoon dried oregano
- 3 tablespoons grated Parmesan cheese
- 2 teaspoons bread machine yeast

**Directions**

**1.  Preparing the Ingredients.**

Choose the size of loaf of your preference and then measure the ingredients.
Add all of the ingredients mentioned previously in the list.
Close the lid after placing the pan in the bread machine.

**2.  Select the Bake cycle**

Turn on the bread machine. Select the White/Basic setting, select the loaf size, and the crust color. Press start.
When the cycle is finished, carefully remove the pan from the bread maker and let it rest.
Remove the bread from the pan, put in a wire rack to Cool about 5 minutes. Slice

# Savory Onion Bread

**PREP: 10 MINUTES /MAKES 1 LOAF**

**Ingredients**

- 12 slice bread (1½ pounds)
- 1 cup water, at 80°F to 90°F
- 3 tablespoons melted butter, cooled
- 1½ tablespoons sugar
- 1⅛ teaspoons salt
- 3 tablespoons dried minced onion
- 1½ tablespoons chopped fresh chives
- 3 cups plus 2 tablespoons white bread flour
- 1⅔ teaspoons bread machine or instant yeast

**Directions**

**1. Preparing the Ingredients.**

Place the ingredients in your bread machine as recommended by the manufacturer.

**2. Select the Bake cycle**

Turn on the bread machine. Select the White/Basic setting, select the loaf size, and the crust color. Press start.

When the cycle is finished, carefully remove the pan from the bread maker and let it rest.

Remove the bread from the pan, put in a wire rack to Cool about 5 minutes. Slice

# Zucchini Spice Bread

**PREP: 10 MINUTES PLUS FERMENTING TIME /MAKES 1 LOAF**

**Ingredients**

- 12 slice bread (1½ pounds)
- 2 eggs, at room temperature
- ½ cup unsalted butter, melted
- ½ teaspoon table salt
- ¾ cup shredded zucchini
- ½ cup light brown sugar
- 2 tablespoons sugar
- 1½ cups all-purpose flour
- ½ teaspoon baking powder
- ½ teaspoon baking soda
- ¼ teaspoon ground allspice
- 1 teaspoon ground cinnamon
- ½ cup chopped pecans

**Directions**

**1. Preparing the Ingredients.**

Choose the size of loaf of your preference and then measure the ingredients.

Add all of the ingredients mentioned previously in the list.

Close the lid after placing the pan in the bread machine.

**2. Select the Bake cycle**

Turn on the bread machine. Select the Quick/Rapid setting, select the loaf size, and the crust color. Press start.

When the cycle is finished, carefully remove the pan from the bread maker and let it rest.

Remove the bread from the pan, put in a wire rack to Cool about 5 minutes. Slice

# Tomato Herb Bread

**PREP: 10 MINUTES /MAKES 1 LOAF**

**Ingredients**
- 8 slice bread (1 pounds)
- ½ cup tomato sauce, at 80°F to 90°F
- ½ tablespoon olive oil
- ½ tablespoon sugar
- 1 tablespoon dried basil
- ½ tablespoon dried oregano
- ½ teaspoon salt
- 2 tablespoons grated Parmesan cheese
- 1½ cups white bread flour
- 1⅛ teaspoons bread machine or instant yeast

**Directions**
1. **Preparing the Ingredients.**
Choose the size of loaf of your preference and then measure the ingredients.
Add all of the ingredients mentioned previously in the list.
Close the lid after placing the pan in the bread machine.
2. **Select the Bake cycle**
Turn on the bread machine. Select the White/Basic setting, select the loaf size, and the crust color. Press start.
When the cycle is finished, carefully remove the pan from the bread maker and let it rest.
Remove the bread from the pan, put in a wire rack to Cool about 5 minutes. Slice

# Potato Honey Bread

**PREP: 10 MINUTES /MAKES 1 LOAF**

**Ingredients**
- 12 slice bread (1½ pounds)
- ¾ cup lukewarm water
- ½ cup finely mashed potatoes, at room temperature
- 1 egg, at room temperature
- ¼ cup unsalted butter, melted
- 2 tablespoons honey
- 1 teaspoon table salt
- 3 cups white bread flour
- 2 teaspoons bread machine yeast

**Directions**
1. **Preparing the Ingredients.**
Choose the size of loaf of your preference and then measure the ingredients.
Add all of the ingredients mentioned previously in the list.
Close the lid after placing the pan in the bread machine.
2. **Select the Bake cycle**

Turn on the bread machine. Select the White/Basic setting, select the loaf size, and the crust color. Press start.

When the cycle is finished, carefully remove the pan from the bread maker and let it rest.

Remove the bread from the pan, put in a wire rack to Cool about 10 minutes. Slice

# Mashed Potato Bread

**PREP: 10 MINUTES /MAKES 1 LOAF**

## Ingredients

- 12 slice bread (1½ pounds)
- ¾ cup water, at 80°F to 90°F
- ½ cup finely mashed potatoes, at room temperature
- 1 egg, at room temperature
- ¼ cup melted butter, cooled
- 2 tablespoons honey
- 1 teaspoon salt
- 3 cups white bread flour
- 2 teaspoons bread machine or instant yeast

## Directions

**1.  Preparing the Ingredients.**

Choose the size of loaf of your preference and then measure the ingredients.

Add all of the ingredients mentioned previously in the list.

Close the lid after placing the pan in the bread machine.

**2.  Select the Bake cycle**

Turn on the bread machine. Select the White/Basic setting, select the loaf size, and the crust color. Press start.

When the cycle is finished, carefully remove the pan from the bread maker and let it rest.

Remove the bread from the pan, put in a wire rack to Cool about 10 minutes. Slice

# Dilly Onion Bread

**PREP: 10 MINUTES /MAKES 14 SLICES**

## Ingredients

¾ cup water (70°F to 80°F)

1 Tbsp butter, softened

2 Tbsp sugar

3 Tbsp dried minced onion

2 Tbsp dried parsley flakes

1 Tbsp dill weed

1 tsp salt

1 garlic clove, minced

2 cups bread flour

⅓ cup whole wheat flour

1 Tbsp nonfat dry milk powder

2 tsp active dry yeast serving

## Directions

**1.  Preparing the Ingredients.**

Add each ingredient to the bread machine in the order and at the temperature recommended by your bread machine manufacturer.

**2. Select the Bake cycle**

Close the lid, select the basic bread, medium crust setting on your bread machine and press start.
When the bread machine has finished baking, remove the bread and put it on a cooling rack.

# Onion Chive Bread

**PREP: 10 MINUTES /MAKES 1 LOAF**

## Ingredients

- 12 slice bread (1½ pounds)
- 1 cup lukewarm water
- 3 tablespoons unsalted butter, melted
- 1½ tablespoons sugar
- 1⅛ teaspoons table salt
- 3⅛ cups white bread flour
- 3 tablespoons dried minced onion
- 1½ tablespoons fresh chives, chopped
- 1⅔ teaspoons bread machine yeast

## Directions

**1. Preparing the Ingredients.**

Choose the size of loaf of your preference and then measure the ingredients.
Add all of the ingredients mentioned previously in the list.
Close the lid after placing the pan in the bread machine.

**2. Select the Bake cycle**

Turn on the bread machine. Select the White/Basic setting, select the loaf size, and the crust color. Press start.
When the cycle is finished, carefully remove the pan from the bread maker and let it rest.
Remove the bread from the pan, put in a wire rack to Cool about 10 minutes. Slice

# Basil Tomato Bread

**PREP: 10 MINUTES /MAKES 14 SLICES**

## Ingredients

- 2¼ tsp dried active baking yeast
- 1⅝ cups bread flour
- 3 Tbsp wheat bran
- 5 Tbsp quinoa
- 3 Tbsp dried milk powder
- 1 Tbsp dried basil
- 25g sun-dried tomatoes, chopped
- 1 tsp salt
- 1⅛ cups water
- 1 cup boiling water to cover tomatoes

## Directions

**1.   Preparing the Ingredients.**

Cover dried tomatoes with boiling water in a bowl.

Soak for 10 minutes, drain, and cool to room temperature.

Snip tomatoes into small pieces, using scissors.

Add each ingredient to the bread machine in the order and at the temperature recommended by your bread machine manufacturer.

**2.   Select the Bake cycle**

Close the lid, select the basic bread, medium crust setting on your bread machine and press start.

When the bread machine has finished baking, remove the bread and put it on a cooling rack.

# Confetti Bread

**PREP: 10 MINUTES /MAKES 1 LOAF**

## Ingredients

- 8 slice bread (1 pounds)
- ⅓ cup milk, at 80°F to 90°F
- 2 tablespoons water, at 80°F to 90°F
- 2 teaspoons melted butter, cooled
- ⅔ teaspoon white vinegar
- 4 teaspoons sugar
- ⅔ teaspoon salt
- 4 teaspoons grated Parmesan cheese
- ⅓ cup quick oats
- 1⅔ cups white bread flour
- 1 teaspoon bread machine or instant yeast
- ⅓ cup finely chopped zucchini
- ¼ cup finely chopped yellow bell pepper
- ¼ cup finely chopped red bell pepper
- 4 teaspoons chopped chives

## Directions

**1.   Preparing the Ingredients.**

Place the ingredients, except the vegetables, in your bread machine as recommended by the manufacturer.

**2.   Select the Bake cycle**

Program the machine for Basic/White bread, select light or medium crust, and press Start.

When the machine signals, add the chopped vegetables; if your machine has no signal, add the vegetables just before the second kneading is finished.

When the cycle is finished, carefully remove the pan from the bread maker and let it rest.

Remove the bread from the pan, put in a wire rack to Cool about 10 minutes. Slice

# Honey Potato Flakes Bread

**PREP: 10 MINUTES /MAKES 1 LOAF**

## Ingredients

- 12 slice bread (1½ pounds)
- 1¼ cups lukewarm milk
- 2 tablespoons unsalted butter, melted

- 1 tablespoon honey
- 1½ teaspoons table salt
- 3 cups white bread flour
- 1 teaspoon dried thyme
- ½ cup instant potato flakes
- 2 teaspoons bread machine yeast

**Directions**
**1.  Preparing the Ingredients.**
Choose the size of loaf of your preference and then measure the ingredients.
Add all of the ingredients mentioned previously in the list.
Close the lid after placing the pan in the bread machine.
**2.  Select the Bake cycle**
Turn on the bread machine. Select the White/Basic setting, select the loaf size, and the crust color. Press start.
When the cycle is finished, carefully remove the pan from the bread maker and let it rest.
Remove the bread from the pan, put in a wire rack to Cool about 10 minutes. Slice

# Pretty Borscht Bread

**PREP: 10 MINUTES /MAKES 1 LOAF**

**Ingredients**
- 12 slice bread (1½ pounds)
- ¾ cups water, at 80°F to 90°F
- ¾ cup grated raw beetroot
- 1½ tablespoons melted butter, cooled
- 1½ tablespoons sugar
- 1¼ teaspoons salt
- 3 cups white bread flour
- 1¼ teaspoons bread machine or instant yeast

**Directions**
**1.  Preparing the Ingredients.**
Place the ingredients in your bread machine as recommended by the manufacturer.
Program the machine for Basic/White bread, select light or medium crust, and press Start.
**2.  Select the Bake cycle**
When the loaf is done, remove the bucket from the machine.
Let the loaf cool for 5 minutes.
Gently shake the bucket to remove the loaf, and turn it out onto a rack to cool.

# Zucchini Lemon Bread

**PREP: 10 MINUTES /MAKES 1 LOAF**

**Ingredients**
- 12 slice bread (1½ pounds)
- ½ cup lukewarm milk
- ¾ cup finely shredded zucchini

- ¼ teaspoon lemon juice, at room temperature
- 1 tablespoon olive oil
- 1 tablespoon sugar
- 1 teaspoon table salt
- ¾ cup whole-wheat flour
- 1½ cups white bread flour
- ¾ cup quick oats
- 2¼ teaspoons bread machine yeast

**Directions**

**1. Preparing the Ingredients.**

Choose the size of loaf of your preference and then measure the ingredients.

Add all of the ingredients mentioned previously in the list.

Close the lid after placing the pan in the bread machine.

**2. Select the Bake cycle**

Turn on the bread machine. Select the White/Basic setting, select the loaf size, and the crust color. Press start.

When the cycle is finished, carefully remove the pan from the bread maker and let it rest.

Remove the bread from the pan, put in a wire rack to Cool about 10 minutes. Slice

# Yeasted Pumpkin Bread

**PREP: 10 MINUTES /MAKES 1 LOAF**

**Ingredients**
- 8 slice bread (1 pounds)
- ⅓ cup milk, at 80°F to 90°F
- ⅔ cup canned pumpkin
- 2 tablespoons melted butter, cooled
- ⅔ teaspoon grated ginger
- 2¾ tablespoons sugar
- ½ teaspoon salt
- ⅔ teaspoon ground cinnamon
- ¼ teaspoon ground cloves
- 2 cups white bread flour
- 1⅛ teaspoons bread machine or instant yeast

**Directions**

**1. Preparing the Ingredients.**

Choose the size of loaf of your preference and then measure the ingredients.

Add all of the ingredients mentioned previously in the list.

Close the lid after placing the pan in the bread machine.

**2. Select the Bake cycle**

Turn on the bread machine. Select the White/Basic setting, select the loaf size, and the crust color. Press start.

When the cycle is finished, carefully remove the pan from the bread maker and let it rest.

Remove the bread from the pan, put in a wire rack to Cool about 10 minutes. Slice

# Oatmeal Zucchini Bread

**PREP: 10 MINUTES /MAKES 1 LOAF**

## Ingredients

- 8 slice bread (1 pounds)
- ⅓ cup milk, at 80°F to 90°F
- ½ cup finely shredded zucchini
- ¼ teaspoon freshly squeezed lemon juice, at room temperature
- 2 teaspoons olive oil
- 2 teaspoons sugar
- ⅔ teaspoon salt
- ½ cup quick oats
- ½ cup whole-wheat flour
- 1 cup white bread flour
- 1½ teaspoons bread machine or instant yeast

## Directions

**1. Preparing the Ingredients.**

Choose the size of loaf of your preference and then measure the ingredients.

Add all of the ingredients mentioned previously in the list.

Close the lid after placing the pan in the bread machine.

**2. Select the Bake cycle**

Turn on the bread machine. Select the White/Basic setting, select the loaf size, and the crust color. Press start.

When the cycle is finished, carefully remove the pan from the bread maker and let it rest.

Remove the bread from the pan, put in a wire rack to Cool about 10 minutes. Slice

# Hot Red Pepper Bread

**PREP: 10 MINUTES /MAKES 1 LOAF**

## Ingredients

- 12 slice bread (1½ pounds)
- 1¼ cups milk, at 80°F to 90°F
- ¼ cup red pepper relish
- 2 tablespoons chopped roasted red pepper
- 3 tablespoons melted butter, cooled
- 3 tablespoons light brown sugar
- 1 teaspoon salt
- 3 cups white bread flour
- 1½ teaspoons bread machine or instant yeast

## Directions

**1. Preparing the Ingredients.**

Choose the size of loaf of your preference and then measure the ingredients.

Add all of the ingredients mentioned previously in the list.

Close the lid after placing the pan in the bread machine.

**2. Select the Bake cycle**

Turn on the bread machine. Select the White/Basic setting, select the loaf size, and the crust color. Press start.

When the cycle is finished, carefully remove the pan from the bread maker and let it rest.

Remove the bread from the pan, put in a wire rack to Cool about 10 minutes. Slice

# French Onion Bread

**PREP: 10 MINUTES /MAKES 1 LOAF**

**Ingredients**

- 12 slice bread (1½ pounds)
- 1¼ cups milk, at 80°F to 90°F
- ¼ cup melted butter, cooled
- 3 tablespoons light brown sugar
- 1 teaspoon salt
- 3 tablespoons dehydrated onion flakes
- 2 tablespoons chopped fresh chives
- 1 teaspoon garlic powder
- 3 cups white bread flour
- 1 teaspoon bread machine or instant yeast

**Directions**

**1. Preparing the Ingredients.**

Choose the size of loaf of your preference and then measure the ingredients.

Add all of the ingredients mentioned previously in the list.

Close the lid after placing the pan in the bread machine.

**2. Select the Bake cycle**

Turn on the bread machine. Select the White/Basic setting, select the loaf size, and the crust color. Press start.

When the cycle is finished, carefully remove the pan from the bread maker and let it rest.

Remove the bread from the pan, put in a wire rack to Cool about 5 minutes. Slice

# Golden Butternut Squash Raisin Bread

**PREP: 10 MINUTES /MAKES 1 LOAF**

**Ingredients**

- 16 slice bread (2 pounds)
- 2 cups cooked mashed butternut squash, at room temperature
- 1 cup (2 sticks) butter, at room temperature
- 3 eggs, at room temperature
- 1 teaspoon pure vanilla extract
- 2 cups sugar
- ½ cup light brown sugar
- 3 cups all-purpose flour
- 1 teaspoon baking soda
- 1 teaspoon ground cinnamon
- ½ teaspoon ground cloves
- ½ teaspoon ground nutmeg

- ½ teaspoon salt
- ½ teaspoon baking powder
- ½ cup golden raisins

**Directions**

**1.  Preparing the Ingredients.**

Place the butternut squash, butter, eggs, vanilla, sugar, and brown sugar in your bread machine.

**2.  Select the Bake cycle**

Program the machine for Quick/Rapid bread and press Start.

While the wet ingredients are mixing, stir together the flour, baking soda, cinnamon, cloves, nutmeg, salt, and baking powder in a small bowl.

After the first fast mixing is done and the machine signals, add the dry ingredients and raisins.

When the cycle is finished, carefully remove the pan from the bread maker and let it rest.

Remove the bread from the pan, put in a wire rack to Cool about 5 minutes. Slice

# Sweet Potato Bread

**PREP: 10 MINUTES /MAKES 1 LOAF**

**Ingredients**

- 12 to 16 slices (1½ to 2 pounds)
- 1½ cups mashed cooked sweet potato, at room temperature
- ¾ cup buttermilk, at room temperature
- ½ cup sugar
- ¼ cup melted butter, cooled
- 1 egg, at room temperature
- 1½ cups all-purpose flour
- 1 teaspoon ground cinnamon
- ½ teaspoon baking powder
- ½ teaspoon baking soda
- ¼ teaspoon ground cloves
- ¼ teaspoon salt

**Directions**

**1.  Preparing the Ingredients.**

Place the sweet potato, buttermilk, sugar, butter, and egg in your bread machine.

**2.  Select the Bake cycle**

Program the machine for Quick/Rapid bread and press Start. While the wet ingredients are mixing, stir together the flour, cinnamon, baking powder, baking soda, cloves, and salt in a small bowl.

After the first fast mixing is done and the machine signals, add the dry ingredients.

When the cycle is finished, carefully remove the pan from the bread maker and let it rest.

Remove the bread from the pan, put in a wire rack to Cool about 5 minutes. Slice

# Potato Thyme Bread

**PREP: 10 MINUTES /MAKES 1 LOAF**

**Ingredients**

- 12 slice bread (1½ pounds)
- 1¼ cups milk, at 80°F to 90°F
- 2 tablespoons melted butter, cooled

- 1 tablespoon honey
- 1½ teaspoons salt
- 1 teaspoon dried thyme
- ½ cup instant potato flakes
- 3 cups white bread flour
- 2 teaspoons bread machine or instant yeast

**Directions**

**1. Preparing the Ingredients.**

Choose the size of loaf of your preference and then measure the ingredients.

Add all of the ingredients mentioned previously in the list.

Close the lid after placing the pan in the bread machine.

**2. Select the Bake cycle**

Turn on the bread machine. Select the White/Basic setting, select the loaf size, and the crust color. Press start.

When the cycle is finished, carefully remove the pan from the bread maker and let it rest.

Remove the bread from the pan, put in a wire rack to Cool about 5 minutes. Slice

# Caramelized Onion Bread

**PREP: 10 MINUTES /MAKES 14 SLICES**

**Ingredients**

- ½ Tbsp butter
- ½ cup onions, sliced
- 1 cup water
- 1 Tbsp olive oil
- 3 cups Gold Medal Better for Bread flour
- 2 Tbsp sugar
- 1 tsp salt
- 1¼ tsp bread machine or quick active dry yeast

**Directions**

**1. Preparing the Ingredients**

Melt the butter over medium-low heat in a skillet.

Cook the onions in the butter for 10 to 15 minutes until they are brown and caramelized - then remove from the heat.

Add each ingredient except the onions to the bread machine in the order and at the temperature recommended by your bread machine manufacturer.

**2. Select the Bake cycle**

Close the lid, select the basic bread, medium crust setting on your bread machine and press start.

Add ½ cup of onions 5 to 10 minutes before the last kneading cycle ends.

When the bread machine has finished baking, remove the bread and put it on a cooling rack.

# Light Corn Bread

**PREP: 10 MINUTES /MAKES 1 LOAF**

**Ingredients**

- 12 slice bread (1½ pounds)
- ¾ cup milk, at 80°F to 90°F
- 1 egg, at room temperature
- 2¼ tablespoons butter, melted and cooled
- 2¼ tablespoons honey
- ¾ teaspoon salt
- ⅓ cup cornmeal
- 2⅔ cups white bread flour
- 1¾ teaspoons bread machine or instant yeast

**Directions**
**1. Preparing the Ingredients.**
Choose the size of loaf of your preference and then measure the ingredients.
Add all of the ingredients mentioned previously in the list.
Close the lid after placing the pan in the bread machine.
**2. Select the Bake cycle**
Turn on the bread machine. Select the White/Basic setting, select the loaf size, and the crust color. Press start.
When the cycle is finished, carefully remove the pan from the bread maker and let it rest.
Remove the bread from the pan, put in a wire rack to Cool about 5 minutes. Slice

# Chive Bread

**PREP: 10 MINUTES /MAKES 14 SLICES**

**Ingredients**
- ⅔ cup milk (70°F to 80°F)
- ¼ cup water (70°F to 80°F)
- ¼ cup sour cream
- 2 Tbsp butter
- 1½ tsp sugar
- 1½ tsp salt
- 3 cups bread flour
- ⅛ tsp baking soda
- ¼ cup minced chives
- 2¼ tsp active dry yeast leaves

**Directions**
**1. Preparing the Ingredients**
Add each ingredient to the bread machine in the order and at the temperature recommended by your bread machine manufacturer.
**2. Select the Bake cycle**
Close the lid, select the basic bread, medium crust setting on your bread machine and press start.
When the bread machine has finished baking, remove the bread and put it on a cooling rack.

# Caramelized Onion Focaccia Bread

**PREP: 10 MINUTES /MAKES 4**

**Ingredients**

- 3/4 cup water
- 2 tablespoons olive oil
- 1 tablespoon sugar
- 1 teaspoon salt
- 2 cups flour
- 1 1/2 teaspoons yeast
- 3/4 cup mozzarella cheese, shredded
- 2 tablespoons parmesan cheese, shredded
- Onion topping:
- 3 tablespoons butter
- 2 medium onions
- 2 cloves garlic, minced

**Directions**

**1. Preparing the Ingredients**

Place all ingredients, except cheese and onion topping, in your bread maker in the order listed above. Grease a large baking sheet. Pat dough into a 12-inch circle on the pan; cover and let rise in warm place for about 30 minutes.

Melt butter in large frying pan over medium-low heat. Cook onions and garlic in butter 15 minutes, stirring often, until onions are caramelized.

Preheat an oven to 400°F.

Make deep depressions across the dough at 1-inch intervals with the handle of a wooden spoon. Spread the onion topping over dough and sprinkle with cheeses.

Bake 15 to 20 minutes or until golden brown. Cut into wedges and serve warm.

# Pumpkin Cinnamon Bread

**PREP: 10 MINUTES /MAKES 14 SLICES**

**Ingredients**

- 1 cup sugar
- 1 cup canned pumpkin
- ⅓ cup vegetable oil
- 1 tsp vanilla
- 2 eggs
- 1½ cups all-purpose bread flour
- 2 tsp baking powder
- ¼ tsp salt
- 1 tsp ground cinnamon
- ¼ tsp ground nutmeg
- ⅛ tsp ground cloves

**Directions**

**1. Preparing the Ingredients**

Add each ingredient to the bread machine in the order and at the temperature recommended by your bread machine manufacturer.

**2. Select the Bake cycle**

Close the lid, select the quick, medium crust setting on your bread machine and press start.
When the bread machine has finished baking, remove the bread and put it on a cooling rack.

# Potato Dill Bread

**PREP: 10 MINUTES /MAKES 14 SLICES**

## Ingredients
- 1 (.25 oz) package active dry yeast
- ½ cup water
- 1 Tbsp sugar
- 1 tsp salt
- 2 Tbsp melted butter
- 1 package or bunch fresh dill
- ¾ cup room temperature mashed potatoes
- 2¼ cups bread flour

## Directions
### 1. Preparing the Ingredients
Add each ingredient to the bread machine in the order and at the temperature recommended by your bread machine manufacturer.
### 2. Select the Bake cycle
Close the lid, select the basic bread, medium crust setting on your bread machine, and press start.
When the bread machine has finished baking, remove the bread and put it on a cooling rack.

# Tomato Basil Bread

**PREP: 10 MINUTES /MAKES 16 SLICES**

## Ingredients
- 3/4 cup warm water
- 1/4 cup fresh basil, minced
- 1/4 cup parmesan cheese, grated
- 3 tablespoons tomato paste
- 1 tablespoon sugar
- 1 tablespoon olive oil
- 1 teaspoon salt
- 1/4 teaspoon crushed red pepper flakes
- 2 1/2 cups bread flour
- 1 package active dry yeast
- Flour, for surface

## Directions
### 1. Preparing the Ingredients
Add ingredients, except yeast, to bread maker pan in above listed order. Make a well in the flour; pour the yeast into the hole.
### 2. Select the Bake cycle
Select Dough cycle and press Start. Turn finished dough out onto a floured surface and knead until

smooth and elastic, about 3 to 5 minutes. Place in a greased bowl, turning once to grease top. Cover and let rise in a warm place until doubled, about 1 hour. Punch dough down and knead for 1 minute. Shape into a round loaf. Place on a greased baking sheet. Cover and let rise until doubled, about 1 hour. With a sharp knife, cut a large "X" in top of loaf. Bake at 375°F for 35-40 minutes or until golden brown. Remove from pan and cool on a cooling rack before serving.

# Zucchini Bread

**PREP: 10 MINUTES /MAKES 12 SLICES**

**Ingredients**
- 1/2 teaspoon salt
- 1 cup sugar
- 1 tablespoon pumpkin pie spice
- 1 tablespoon baking powder
- 1 teaspoon pure vanilla extract
- 1/3 cup milk
- 1/2 cup vegetable oil
- 2 eggs
- 2 cups bread flour
- 1 1/2 teaspoons active dry yeast or bread machine yeast
- 1 cup shredded zucchini, raw and unpeeled
- 1 cup of chopped walnuts (optional)

**Directions**

**1.  Preparing the Ingredients**

Add all of the ingredients for the zucchini bread into the bread maker pan in the order listed above, reserving yeast.

Make a well in the center of the dry ingredients and add the yeast.

**2.  Select the Bake cycle**

Select Wheat bread cycle, medium crust color, and press Start.

Transfer to a cooling rack for 10 to 15 minutes before slicing to serve.

# Gluten-Free Pumpkin Pie Bread

**PREP: 5 MINUTES /MAKES 12 SLICES**

**Ingredients**
- 1/4 cup olive oil
- 2 large eggs, beaten
- 1 tablespoon bourbon vanilla extract
- 1 cup canned pumpkin
- 4 tablespoons honey
- 1/4 teaspoon lemon juice
- 1/2 cup buckwheat flour
- 1/4 cup millet flour
- 1/4 cup sorghum flour
- 1/2 cup tapioca starch

- 1 cup light brown sugar
- 2 teaspoons baking powder
- 1 teaspoon baking soda
- 1/2 teaspoon sea salt
- 1 teaspoon xanthan gum
- 1 teaspoon ground cinnamon
- 1 teaspoon allspice
- 1-2 tablespoons peach juice

**Directions**

**1. Preparing the Ingredients**

Mix dry ingredients together in a bowl and put aside.

Add wet ingredients to pan, except peach juice.

Add mixed dry ingredients to bread maker pan.

**2. Select the Bake cycle**

Set to Sweet bread cycle, light or medium crust color, and press Start.

As it begins to mix the ingredients, use a soft silicone spatula to scrape down the sides.

If the batter is stiff, add one tablespoon at a time of peach juice until the batter becomes slightly thinner than muffin batter.

Close the lid and allow to bake. Remove to a cooling rack for 20 minutes before slicing .

# CHEESE BREADS

## Zesty Cheddar Bread

**PREP: 10 MINUTES /MAKES 1 LOAF**

**Ingredients**
- 12 slice bread (1½ pounds)
- 1 cup buttermilk
- 1/3 cup butter, melted
- 1 tablespoon sugar
- 2 tablespoons finely chopped chipotle chiles in adobo sauce (from 7-oz can) 2 eggs
- 2 cups all-purpose flour
- 1 cup shredded Cheddar cheese (4 oz)
- 2 teaspoons baking powder
- 1 teaspoon baking soda
- ½ teaspoon salt

**Directions**

**1. Preparing the Ingredients.**

Choose the size of loaf of your preference and then measure the ingredients.

Add all of the ingredients mentioned previously in the list.

Close the lid after placing the pan in the bread machine.

**2. Select the Bake cycle**

Turn on the bread machine. Select the White/Basic setting, select the loaf size, and the crust color. Press start.

When the cycle is finished, carefully remove the pan from the bread maker and let it rest.

Remove the bread from the pan, put in a wire rack to Cool about 5 minutes. Serve warm

# French Cheese Bread

**PREP: 10 MINUTES /MAKES 14 SLICES**

**Ingredients**
- 1 tsp sugar
- 2¼ tsp yeast
- 1¼ cup water
- 3 cups bread flour
- 2 Tbsp parmesan cheese
- 1 tsp garlic powder
- 1½ tsp salt

**Directions**

**1.  Preparing the Ingredients**

Add each ingredient to the bread machine in the order and at the temperature recommended by your bread machine manufacturer.

**2.  Select the Bake cycle**

Close the lid, select the basic bread, medium crust setting on your bread machine, and press start.

When the bread machine has finished baking, remove the bread and put it on a cooling rack.

# Romano Oregano Bread

**PREP: 10 MINUTES /MAKES 1 LOAF**

**Ingredients**
- 12 slice bread (1½ pounds)
- 1 cup lukewarm water
- 3 tablespoons sugar
- 1½ tablespoons olive oil
- 1 teaspoon table salt
- 1 tablespoon dried leaf oregano
- ½ cup cheese (Romano or Parmesan), freshly grated
- 3 cups white bread flour
- 2 teaspoons bread machine yeast

**Directions**

**1.  Preparing the Ingredients.**

Choose the size of loaf of your preference and then measure the ingredients.

Add all of the ingredients mentioned previously in the list.

Close the lid after placing the pan in the bread machine.

**2.  Select the Bake cycle**

Turn on the bread machine. Select the White/Basic setting, select the loaf size, and the crust color. Press start.

When the cycle is finished, carefully remove the pan from the bread maker and let it rest.

Remove the bread from the pan, put in a wire rack to Cool about 5 minutes. Slice

# Jalapeno Cheese Bread

## Ingredients

- 3 cups bread flour
- 1½ tsp active dry yeast
- 1 cup water
- 2 Tbsp sugar
- 1 tsp salt
- ½ cup shredded cheddar cheese
- ¼ cup diced jalapeno peppers

## Directions

**1. Preparing the Ingredients.**

Add each ingredient to the bread machine in the order and at the temperature recommended by your bread machine manufacturer.

**2. Select the Bake cycle**

Close the lid, select the basic bread, medium crust setting on your bread machine, and press start. When the bread machine has finished baking, remove the bread and put it on a cooling rack.

# Cheesy Chipotle Bread

**PREP: 10 MINUTES /MAKES 1 LOAF**

## Ingredients

- 8 slice bread (1 pounds)
- ⅔ cup water, at 80°F to 90°F
- 1½ tablespoons sugar
- 1½ tablespoons powdered skim milk
- ¾ teaspoon salt
- ½ teaspoon chipotle chili powder
- 2 cups white bread flour
- ½ cup (2 ounces) shredded sharp Cheddar cheese
- ¾ teaspoon bread machine or instant yeast

## Directions

**1. Preparing the Ingredients.**

Choose the size of loaf of your preference and then measure the ingredients.

Add all of the ingredients mentioned previously in the list.

Close the lid after placing the pan in the bread machine.

**2. Select the Bake cycle**

Turn on the bread machine. Select the White/Basic setting, select the loaf size, and the crust color. Press start.

When the cycle is finished, carefully remove the pan from the bread maker and let it rest.

Remove the bread from the pan, put in a wire rack to Cool about 5 minutes. Slice

# Cheddar Cheese Bread

**PREP: 10 MINUTES /MAKES 1 LOAF**

**Ingredients**
- 1 cup lukewarm milk
- 3 cups all-purpose flour
- 1¼ tsp salt
- 1 tsp tabasco sauce, optional
- ¼ cup Vermont cheese powder
- 1 Tbsp sugar
- 1 cup grated cheddar cheese, firmly packed
- 1½ tsp instant yeast

**Directions**

**1.  Preparing the Ingredients**

Add each ingredient to the bread machine in the order and at the temperature recommended by your bread machine manufacturer.

**2.  Select the Bake cycle**

Close the lid, select the basic bread, medium crust setting on your bread machine, and press start. When the bread machine has finished baking, remove the bread and put it on a cooling rack.

# Apricot–Cream Cheese Ring

**PREP: 10 MINUTES /MAKES 10 SERVINGS**

**Ingredients**
- 1/3 cup water
- 2 tablespoons butter, softened
- 1 egg
- 2 cups bread flour
- 2 tablespoons sugar
- ½ teaspoon salt
- 1¾ teaspoons bread machine or fast-acting dry yeast
- filling
- 1 package (3 oz) cream cheese, softened
- 1½ tablespoons bread flour
- ¼ cup apricot preserves
- 1 egg, beaten
- 2 tablespoons sliced almonds

**Directions**

**1.  Preparing the Ingredients.**

Measure carefully, placing all bread dough ingredients in bread machine pan in the order recommended by the manufacturer.

Select Dough/Manual cycle. Do not use delay cycle.

Remove dough from pan, using lightly floured hands. Cover and let rest 10 minutes on lightly floured surface. In small bowl, mix cream cheese and 1½ tablespoons flour.

4 Grease 9-inch round pan with shortening. Roll dough into 15-inch round.

Place in pan, letting side of dough hang over edge of pan. Spread cream cheese mixture over dough in pan; spoon apricot preserves onto cream cheese mixture.

**2.  Select the Bake cycle**

Make cuts along edge of dough at 1-inch intervals to about ½ inch above cream cheese mixture. Twist

pairs of dough strips and fold over cream cheese mixture.
Cover and let rise in warm place 40 to 50 minutes or until almost double.
5 Heat oven to 375°F. Brush beaten egg over dough. Sprinkle with  almonds.
Bake 30 to 35 minutes or until golden brown. Cool at least 30 minutes before cutting.

# Cottage Cheese and Chive Bread

**PREP: 10 MINUTES /MAKES 14 SERVINGS**

**Ingredients**
- ⅜ cup water
- 1 cup cottage cheese
- 1 large egg
- 2 Tbsp butter
- 1½ tsp salt
- 3¾ cups white bread flour
- 3 Tbsp dried chives
- 2½ Tbsp granulated sugar
- 2¼ tsp active dry yeast

**Directions**
**1.  Preparing the Ingredients**
Add each ingredient to the bread machine in the order and at the temperature recommended by your bread machine manufacturer.
**2.  Select the Bake cycle**
Close the lid, select the basic bread, medium crust setting on your bread machine, and press start.
When the bread machine has finished baking, remove the bread and put it on a cooling rack.

# Mexican Style Jalapeno Cheese Bread

**PREP: 10 MINUTES /MAKES 1 LOAF**

**Ingredients**
- 12 slice bread (1½ pounds)
- 1 small jalapeno pepper, seeded and minced
- ¾ cup lukewarm water
- 2 tablespoons nonfat dry milk powder
- 1 tablespoon unsalted butter, melted
- 1 tablespoon sugar
- 1 teaspoon salt
- 3 tablespoons finely shredded cheese (Mexican blend or Monterrey Jack)
- 2 cups white bread flour
- 1½ teaspoons bread machine yeast

**Directions**
**1.  Preparing the Ingredients.**
Choose the size of loaf of your preference and then measure the ingredients.
Add all of the ingredients mentioned previously in the list.
Close the lid after placing the pan in the bread machine.

**2. Select the Bake cycle**

Turn on the bread machine. Select the White/Basic setting, select the loaf size, and the crust color. Press start.

When the cycle is finished, carefully remove the pan from the bread maker and let it rest.

Remove the bread from the pan, put in a wire rack to Cool about 5 minutes. Slice

# Ricotta Bread

**PREP: 10 MINUTES /MAKES 14 SLICES**

## Ingredients

- 3 Tbsp skim milk
- ⅔ cup ricotta cheese
- 4 tsp unsalted butter, softened to room temperature
- 1 large egg
- 2 Tbsp granulated sugar
- ½ tsp salt
- 1½ cups bread flour, + more flour, as needed
- 1 tsp active dry yeast

## Directions

**1. Preparing the Ingredients**

Add each ingredient to the bread machine in the order and at the temperature recommended by your bread machine manufacturer.

**2. Select the Bake cycle**

Close the lid, select the basic bread, medium crust setting on your bread machine, and press start.

When the bread machine has finished baking, remove the bread and put it on a cooling rack .

# Roasted Garlic Asiago Bread

**PREP: 10 MINUTES /MAKES 1 LOAF**

## Ingredients

- 12 slice bread (1½ pounds)
- ¾ cup plus 1 tablespoon milk, at 70°F to 80°F
- ¼ cup melted butter, cooled
- 1 teaspoon minced garlic
- 2 tablespoons sugar
- 1 teaspoon salt
- ½ cup (2 ounces) grated Asiago cheese
- 2¾ cups white bread flour
- 1½ teaspoons bread machine or instant yeast
- ½ cup mashed roasted garlic

## Directions

**1. Preparing the Ingredients.**

Choose the size of loaf of your preference and then measure the ingredients.

Add all of the ingredients mentioned previously in the list.

Close the lid after placing the pan in the bread machine.

**2. Select the Bake cycle**

Turn on the bread machine. Select the White/Basic setting, select the loaf size, and the crust color. Press start.

When the cycle is finished, carefully remove the pan from the bread maker and let it rest.

Remove the bread from the pan, put in a wire rack to Cool about 5 minutes. Slice

# Jalapeno Cheddar Bread

**PREP: 10 MINUTES /MAKES 1 LOAF**

**Ingredients**

- 12 slice bread (1½ pounds)
- 1 cup lukewarm buttermilk
- ¼ cup unsalted butter, melted
- 2 eggs, at room temperature
- ½ teaspoon table salt
- 1 jalapeno pepper, chopped
- ½ cup Cheddar cheese, shredded
- ¼ cup sugar
- 1⅓ cups all-purpose flour
- 1 cup cornmeal
- 1 tablespoon baking powder

**Directions**

**1. Preparing the Ingredients.**

Choose the size of loaf of your preference and then measure the ingredients.

Add all of the ingredients mentioned previously in the list.

Close the lid after placing the pan in the bread machine.

**2. Select the Bake cycle**

Turn on the bread machine. Select the Rapid/Quick setting, select the loaf size, and the crust color. Press start.

When the cycle is finished, carefully remove the pan from the bread maker and let it rest.

Remove the bread from the pan, put in a wire rack to Cool about 5 minutes. Slice

# Oregano Cheese Bread

**PREP: 10 MINUTES /MAKES 1 LOAF**

**Ingredients**

- 3 cups bread flour
- 1 cup water
- ½ cup freshly grated parmesan cheese
- 3 Tbsp sugar
- 1 Tbsp dried leaf oregano
- 1½ Tbsp olive oil
- 1 tsp salt
- 2 tsp active dry yeast

**Directions**

**1. Preparing the Ingredients**

Add each ingredient to the bread machine in the order and at the temperature recommended by your bread machine manufacturer.

**2.  Select the Bake cycle**

Close the lid, select the basic bread, medium crust setting on your bread machine, and press start.

When the bread machine has finished baking, remove the bread and put it on a cooling rack.

# Cheddar Cheese Basil Bread

PREP: 10 MINUTES /MAKES 1 LOAF

## Ingredients

- 12 slice bread (1½ pounds)
- 1 cup milk, at 80°F to 90°F
- 1 tablespoon melted butter, cooled
- 1 tablespoon sugar
- 1 teaspoon dried basil
- ¾ cup (3 ounces) shredded sharp Cheddar cheese
- ¾ teaspoon salt
- 3 cups white bread flour
- 1½ teaspoons bread machine or active dry yeast

## Directions

**1.  Preparing the Ingredients.**

Choose the size of loaf of your preference and then measure the ingredients.

Add all of the ingredients mentioned previously in the list.

Close the lid after placing the pan in the bread machine.

**2.  Select the Bake cycle**

Turn on the bread machine. Select the White/Basic setting, select the loaf size, and the crust color. Press start.

When the cycle is finished, carefully remove the pan from the bread maker and let it rest.

Remove the bread from the pan, put in a wire rack to Cool about 5 minutes. Slice

# Spinach and Feta Bread

PREP: 10 MINUTES /MAKES 14 SLICES

## Ingredients

- 1 cup water
- 2 tsp butter
- 3 cups flour
- 1 tsp sugar
- 2 tsp instant minced onion
- 1 tsp salt
- 1¼ tsp instant yeast
- 1 cup crumbled feta
- 1 cup chopped fresh spinach leaves

## Directions

*1.  Preparing the Ingredients*

Add each ingredient except the cheese and spinach to the bread machine in the order and at the temperature recommended by your bread machine manufacturer.

**2. Select the Bake cycle**

Close the lid, select the basic bread, medium crust setting on your bread machine, and press start.

When only 10 minutes are left in the last kneading cycle add the spinach and cheese.

When the bread machine has finished baking, remove the bread and put it on a cooling rack.

# Blue Cheese Bread

**PREP: 10 MINUTES /MAKES 12 SLICES**

**Ingredients**
- 3/4 cup warm water
- 1 large egg
- 1 teaspoon salt
- 3 cups bread flour
- 1 cup blue cheese, crumbled
- 2 tablespoons nonfat dry milk
- 2 tablespoons sugar
- 1 teaspoon bread machine yeast

**Directions**

### 1. Preparing the Ingredients

Add the ingredients to bread machine pan in the order listed above, (except yeast) ; be sure to add the cheese with the flour.

Make a well in the flour; pour the yeast into the hole.

**2. Select the Bake cycle**

Select Basic bread cycle, medium crust color, and press Start.

When finished, transfer to a cooling rack for 10 minutes and serve warm.

# Parsley Garlic Bread

**PREP: 10 MINUTES /MAKES 1 LOAF**

**Ingredients**
- 12 slice bread (1½ pounds)
- 1 cup lukewarm milk
- 1½ tablespoons unsalted butter, melted
- 1 tablespoon sugar
- 1½ teaspoons table salt
- 2 teaspoons garlic powder
- 2 teaspoons fresh parsley, chopped
- 3 cups white bread flour
- 1¾ teaspoons bread machine yeast

**Directions**

**1. Preparing the Ingredients.**

Choose the size of loaf of your preference and then measure the ingredients.

Add all of the ingredients mentioned previously in the list.

Close the lid after placing the pan in the bread machine.

**2. Select the Bake cycle**

Turn on the bread machine. Select the White/Basic setting, select the loaf size, and the crust color. Press start.

When the cycle is finished, carefully remove the pan from the bread maker and let it rest.
Remove the bread from the pan, put in a wire rack to Cool about 10 minutes. Slice

# Prosciutto Parmesan Breadsticks

**PREP: 10 MINUTES /MAKES 12**

**Ingredients**

- 1 1/3 cups warm water
- 1 tablespoon butter
- 1 1/2 tablespoons sugar
- 1 1/2 teaspoons salt
- 4 cups bread flour
- 2 teaspoons yeast
- For the topping:
- 1/2 pound prosciutto, sliced very thin
- 1/2 cup of grated parmesan cheese
- 1 egg yolk
- 1 tablespoon of water

**Directions**

**1. Preparing the Ingredients**

Place the first set of dough ingredients (except yeast) in the bread pan in the order indicated. Do not add any of the topping ingredients yet. Make a well in the center of the dry ingredients and add the yeast.

**2. Select the Bake cycle**

Select the Dough cycle on the bread machine. When finished, drop the dough onto a lightly-floured surface.

Roll the dough out flat to about 1/4-inch thick, or about half a centimeter. Cover with plastic wrap and let rise for 20 to 30 minutes.

Sprinkle dough evenly with parmesan and carefully lay the prosciutto slices on the surface of the dough to cover as much of it as possible. Preheat an oven to 400°F.

Cut the dough into 12 long strips, about one inch wide. Twist each end in opposite directions, twisting the toppings into the bread stick. Place the breadsticks onto a lightly greased baking sheet. Whisk the egg yolk and water together in a small mixing bowl and lightly baste each breadstick. Bake for 8 to 10 minutes or until golden brown.

Remove from oven and serve warm.

# Jalapeño Corn Bread

**PREP: 10 MINUTES /MAKES 1 LOAF**

**Ingredients**

- 12 to 16 slices bread (1½ to 2 pounds)
- 1 cup buttermilk, at 80°F to 90°F
- ¼ cup melted butter, cooled
- 2 eggs, at room temperature
- 1 jalapeño pepper, chopped
- 1⅓ cups all-purpose flour
- 1 cup cornmeal
- ½ cup (2 ounces) shredded Cheddar cheese
- ¼ cup sugar

- 1 tablespoon baking powder
- ½ teaspoon salt

**Directions**
**1.  Preparing the Ingredients.**
Choose the size of loaf of your preference and then measure the ingredients.
Add all of the ingredients mentioned previously in the list.
Close the lid after placing the pan in the bread machine.
**2.  Select the Bake cycle**
Turn on the bread machine. Select the Quick/Rapid setting, select the loaf size, and the crust color. Press start.
When the cycle is finished, carefully remove the pan from the bread maker and let it rest.
Remove the bread from the pan, put in a wire rack to Cool about 5 minutes. Slice

# Cheddar Bacon Bread

**PREP: 10 MINUTES /MAKES 1 LOAF**

**Ingredients**
- 12 slice bread (1½ pounds)
- ½ cup lukewarm milk
- 1½ teaspoons unsalted butter, melted
- 1½ tablespoons honey
- 1½ teaspoons table salt
- ½ cup green chilies, chopped
- ½ cup grated Cheddar cheese
- ½ cup cooked bacon, chopped
- 3 cups white bread flour
- 2 teaspoons bread machine yeast

**Directions**
**1.  Preparing the Ingredients.**
Choose the size of loaf of your preference and then measure the ingredients.
Add all of the ingredients mentioned previously in the list.
Close the lid after placing the pan in the bread machine.
**2.  Select the Bake cycle**
Turn on the bread machine. Select the White/Basic setting, select the loaf size, and the crust color. Press start.
When the cycle is finished, carefully remove the pan from the bread maker and let it rest.
Remove the bread from the pan, put in a wire rack to Cool about 5 minutes. Slice

# Italian Cheese Bread

**PREP: 10 MINUTES /MAKES 14 SLICES**

**Ingredients**
- 1¼ cups water
- 3 cups bread flour

- ½ shredded pepper jack cheese
- 2 tsp Italian seasoning
- 2 Tbsp brown sugar
- 1½ tsp salt
- 2 tsp active dry yeast

**Directions**

**1. Preparing the Ingredients.**

Add each ingredient to the bread machine in the order and at the temperature recommended by your bread machine manufacturer.

**2. Select the Bake cycle**

Close the lid, select the basic bread, medium crust setting on your bread machine, and press start.

When the bread machine has finished baking, remove the bread and put it on a cooling rack.

# Olive Cheese Bread

**PREP: 10 MINUTES /MAKES 1 LOAF**

**Ingredients**
- 12 slice bread (1½ pounds)
- 1 cup milk, at 80°F to 90°F
- 1½ tablespoons melted butter, cooled
- 1 teaspoon minced garlic
- 1½ tablespoons sugar
- 1 teaspoon salt
- 3 cups white bread flour
- ¾ cup (3 ounces) shredded Swiss cheese
- 1 teaspoon bread machine or instant yeast
- ⅓ cup chopped black olives

**Directions**

**1. Preparing the Ingredients.**

Place the ingredients in your bread machine as recommended by the manufacturer, tossing the flour with the cheese first.

**2. Select the Bake cycle**

Program the machine for Basic/White bread, select light or medium crust, and press Start.

When the cycle is finished, carefully remove the pan from the bread maker and let it rest.

Remove the bread from the pan, put in a wire rack to Cool about 10 minutes. Slice

# Cheesy Sausage Loaf

**PREP: 10 MINUTES /MAKES 1 LOAF**

**Ingredients**
- 1 cup warm water
- 4 teaspoons butter, softened
- 1 1/4 teaspoons salt
- 1 teaspoon sugar
- 3 cups bread flour

- 2 1/4 teaspoons active dry yeast
- 1 pound pork sausage roll, cooked and drained
- 1 1/2 cups Italian cheese, shredded
- 1/4 teaspoon garlic powder
- Pinch of black pepper
- 1 egg, lightly beaten
- Flour, for surface

**Directions**

**1.  Preparing the Ingredients**

Add the first five ingredients to the bread maker pan in order listed above.

Make a well in the flour; pour the yeast into the hole.

**2.  Select the Bake cycle**

Select Dough cycle and press Start.

Turn kneaded dough onto a lightly floured surface and roll into a 16-by-10-inch rectangle. Cover with plastic wrap and let rest for 10 minutes Combine sausage, cheese, garlic powder and pepper in a mixing bowl.

Spread sausage mixture evenly over the dough to within one 1/2 inch of edges. Start with a long side and roll up like a jelly roll, pinch seams to seal, and tuck ends under. Place the loaf seam-side down on a greased baking sheet. Cover and let rise in a warm place for 30 minutes. Preheat an oven to 350°F and bake 20 minutes. Brush with egg and bake an additional 15 to 20 minutes until golden brown. Remove to a cooling rack and serve warm.

# Mixed Herb Cheese Bread

**PREP: 10 MINUTES PLUS FERMENTING TIME/MAKES 1 LOAF**

**Ingredients**

- 12 slice bread (1½ pounds)
- 1 cup lukewarm water
- 1½ tablespoons olive oil
- ¾ teaspoon table salt
- ¾ tablespoon sugar
- 2 cloves garlic, crushed
- 2 tablespoons mixed fresh herbs (basil, chives, oregano, rosemary, etc.)
- 3 tablespoons Parmesan cheese, grated
- 3 cups white bread flour
- 1⅔ teaspoons bread machine yeast

**Directions**

**1.  Preparing the Ingredients.**

Choose the size of loaf of your preference and then measure the ingredients.

Add all of the ingredients mentioned previously in the list.

Close the lid after placing the pan in the bread machine.

**2.  Select the Bake cycle**

Turn on the bread machine. Select the White/Basic setting, select the loaf size, and the crust color. Press start.

When the cycle is finished, carefully remove the pan from the bread maker and let it rest.

Remove the bread from the pan, put in a wire rack to Cool about 5 minutes. Slice

# Blue Cheese Onion Bread

**PREP: 10 MINUTE S PLUS FERMENTING TIME /MAKES 1 LOAF**

## Ingredients

- 12 slice bread (1½ pounds)
- 1¼ cup water, at 80°F to 90°F
- 1 egg, at room temperature
- 1 tablespoon melted butter, cooled
- ¼ cup powdered skim milk
- 1 tablespoon sugar
- ¾ teaspoon salt
- ½ cup (2 ounces) crumbled blue cheese
- 1 tablespoon dried onion flakes
- 3 cups white bread flour
- ¼ cup instant mashed potato flakes
- 1 teaspoon bread machine or active dry yeast

## Directions

**1. Preparing the Ingredients.**

Choose the size of loaf of your preference and then measure the ingredients.

Add all of the ingredients mentioned previously in the list.

Close the lid after placing the pan in the bread machine.

**2. Select the Bake cycle**

Turn on the bread machine. Select the Quick/Rapid setting, select the loaf size, and the crust color. Press start.

When the cycle is finished, carefully remove the pan from the bread maker and let it rest.

Remove the bread from the pan, put in a wire rack to Cool about 10 minutes. Slice

# Cheddar and Bacon Bread

**PREP: 10 MINUTE S PLUS FERMENTING TIME /MAKES 14 SLICES**

## Ingredients

- 1⅓ cups water
- 2 Tbsp vegetable oil
- 1¼ tsp salt
- 2 Tbsp plus 1½ tsp sugar
- 4 cups bread flour
- 3 Tbsp nonfat dry milk
- 2 tsp dry active yeast
- 2 cups cheddar
- 8 slices crumbled bacon

## Directions

**1. Preparing the Ingredients**

Add each ingredient to the bread machine except the cheese and bacon in the order and at the temperature recommended by your bread machine manufacturer.

**2. Select the Bake cycle**

Close the lid, select the basic bread, medium crust setting on your bread machine, and press start.

Add the cheddar cheese and bacon 30 to 40 minutes into the cycle. When the bread machine has finished baking, remove the bread and put it on a cooling rack .

# Basil Cheese Bread

**PREP: 10 MINUTE S PLUS FERMENTING TIME /MAKES 1 LOAF**

## Ingredients

- 12 slice bread (1½ pounds)
- 1 cup lukewarm milk
- 1 tablespoon unsalted butter, melted
- 1 tablespoon sugar
- 1 teaspoon dried basil
- ¾ teaspoon table salt
- ¾ cup sharp Cheddar cheese, shredded
- 3 cups white bread flour
- 1½ teaspoons bread machine yeast

## Directions

*1. Preparing the Ingredients.*

Choose the size of loaf of your preference and then measure the ingredients.

Add all of the ingredients mentioned previously in the list.

Close the lid after placing the pan in the bread machine.

**2. Select the Bake cycle**

Turn on the bread machine. Select the Quick/Rapid setting, select the loaf size, and the crust color. Press start.

When the cycle is finished, carefully remove the pan from the bread maker and let it rest.

Remove the bread from the pan, put in a wire rack to Cool about 5 minutes. Slice

# Double Cheese Bread

**PREP: 10 MINUTES PLUS FERMENTING TIME/MAKES 1 LOAF**

## Ingredients

- 8 slices bread (1 pound)
- ¾ cup plus 1 tablespoon milk, at 80°F to 90°F
- 2 teaspoons butter, melted and cooled
- 4 teaspoons sugar
- ⅔ teaspoon salt
- ⅓ teaspoon freshly ground black pepper
- Pinch cayenne pepper
- 1 cup (4 ounces) shredded aged sharp Cheddar cheese
- ⅓ cup shredded or grated Parmesan cheese
- 2 cups white bread flour
- ¾ teaspoon bread machine or instant yeast

**Directions**

**1. Preparing the Ingredients.**

Choose the size of loaf of your preference and then measure the ingredients.

Add all of the ingredients mentioned previously in the list.

Close the lid after placing the pan in the bread machine.

**2. Select the Bake cycle**

Turn on the bread machine. Select the Quick/Rapid setting, select the loaf size, and the crust color. Press start.

When the cycle is finished, carefully remove the pan from the bread maker and let it rest.

Remove the bread from the pan, put in a wire rack to Cool about 5 minutes. Slice

# American Cheese Beer Bread

**PREP: 10 MINUTE S PLUS FERMENTING TIME /MAKES 1 LOAF**

**Ingredients**

- 16 slice bread (2 pounds)
- 1⅔ cups warm beer
- 1½ tablespoons sugar
- 2 teaspoons table salt
- 1½ tablespoons unsalted butter, melted
- ¾ cup American cheese, shredded
- ¾ cup Monterrey Jack cheese, shredded
- 4 cups white bread flour
- 2 teaspoons bread machine yeast

**Directions**

**1. Preparing the Ingredients.**

Choose the size of loaf of your preference and then measure the ingredients.

Add all of the ingredients mentioned previously in the list.

Close the lid after placing the pan in the bread machine.

**2. Select the Bake cycle**

Turn on the bread machine. Select the Quick/Rapid setting, select the loaf size, and the crust color. Press start.

When the cycle is finished, carefully remove the pan from the bread maker and let it rest.

Remove the bread from the pan, put in a wire rack to Cool about 5 minutes. Slice

# Mozzarella and Salami Bread

**PREP: 10 MINUTE S PLUS FERMENTING TIME /MAKES 1 LOAF**

**Ingredients**

- 12 slice bread (1½ pounds)
- 1 cup water plus 2 tablespoons, at 80°F to 90°F
- ½ cup (2 ounces) shredded mozzarella cheese
- 2 tablespoons sugar
- 1 teaspoon salt
- 1 teaspoon dried basil

- ¼ teaspoon garlic powder
- 3¼ cups white bread flour
- 1½ teaspoons bread machine or instant yeast
- ¾ cup finely diced hot German salami

**Directions**

**1. Preparing the Ingredients.**
- Place the ingredients, except the salami, in your bread machine as recommended by the manufacturer.
- Program the machine for Basic/White bread, select light or medium crust, and press Start.
- When the loaf is done, remove the bucket from the machine.

**2. Select the Bake cycle**
- Add the salami when your machine signals or 5 minutes before the second kneading cycle is finished.

Let the loaf cool for 5 minutes. Gently shake the bucket to remove the loaf, and turn it out onto a rack to cool.

# Simple Cottage Cheese Bread

**PREP: 10 MINUTES PLUS FERMENTING TIME /MAKES 1 LOAF**

**Ingredients**
- 12 slice bread (1½ pounds)
- ½ cup water, at 80°F to 90°F
- ¾ cup cottage cheese, at room temperature
- 1 egg, at room temperature
- 2 tablespoons butter, melted and cooled
- 1 tablespoon sugar
- 1 teaspoon salt
- ¼ teaspoon baking soda
- 3 cups white bread flour
- 2 teaspoons bread machine or instant yeast

**Directions**

**1. Preparing the Ingredients.**
Choose the size of loaf of your preference and then measure the ingredients.
Add all of the ingredients mentioned previously in the list.
Close the lid after placing the pan in the bread machine.

**2. Select the Bake cycle**
Turn on the bread machine. Select the White/Basic setting, select the loaf size, and the crust color. Press start.
When the cycle is finished, carefully remove the pan from the bread maker and let it rest.

Remove the bread from the pan, put in a wire rack to Cool about 5 minutes. Slice

# Parmesan Cheddar Bread

**PREP: 10 MINUTES PLUS FERMENTING TIME /MAKES 1 LOAF**

**Ingredients**

- 12 slice bread (1½ pounds)
- 1¼ cups lukewarm milk
- 1 tablespoon unsalted butter, melted
- 2 tablespoons sugar
- 1 teaspoon table salt
- ½ teaspoon freshly ground black pepper
- Pinch cayenne pepper
- 1½ cups shredded aged sharp Cheddar cheese
- ½ cup shredded or grated Parmesan cheese
- 3 cups white bread flour
- 1¼ teaspoons bread machine yeast

## Directions

### 1. Preparing the Ingredients.

Choose the size of loaf of your preference and then measure the ingredients.

Add all of the ingredients mentioned previously in the list.

Close the lid after placing the pan in the bread machine.

### 2. Select the Bake cycle

Turn on the bread machine. Select the Quick/Rapid setting, select the loaf size, and the crust color. Press start.

When the cycle is finished, carefully remove the pan from the bread maker and let it rest.

Remove the bread from the pan, put in a wire rack to Cool about 5 minutes. Slice

# Chile Cheese Bacon Bread

**PREP: 10 MINUTES PLUS FERMENTING TIME /MAKES 1 LOAF**

## Ingredients

- 8 slices bread (1 pound)
- ⅓ cup milk, at 80°F to 90°F
- 1 teaspoon melted butter, cooled
- 1 tablespoon honey
- 1 teaspoon salt
- ⅓ cup chopped and drained green chiles
- ⅓ cup grated Cheddar cheese
- ⅓ cup chopped cooked bacon
- 2 cups white bread flour
- 1⅓ teaspoons bread machine or instant yeast

## Directions

### 1. Preparing the Ingredients.

Choose the size of loaf of your preference and then measure the ingredients.

Add all of the ingredients mentioned previously in the list.

Close the lid after placing the pan in the bread machine.

### 2. Select the Bake cycle

Turn on the bread machine. Select the Quick/Rapid setting, select the loaf size, and the crust color. Press start.

When the cycle is finished, carefully remove the pan from the bread maker and let it rest.

Remove the bread from the pan, put in a wire rack to Cool about 5 minutes. Slice

# Honey Goat Cheese Bread

**PREP: 10 MINUTES PLUS FERMENTING TIME /MAKES 1 LOAF**

## Ingredients

- 12 slice bread (1½ pounds)
- 1 cup lukewarm milk
- 1½ tablespoons honey
- 1 teaspoon table salt
- 1 teaspoon freshly cracked black pepper
- ¼ cup goat cheese, shredded or crumbled
- 3 cups white bread flour
- 1½ teaspoons bread machine yeast

## Directions

**1.  Preparing the Ingredients.**

Choose the size of loaf of your preference and then measure the ingredients.

Add all of the ingredients mentioned previously in the list.

Close the lid after placing the pan in the bread machine.

**2.  Select the Bake cycle**

Turn on the bread machine. Select the Quick/Rapid setting, select the loaf size, and the crust color. Press start.

When the cycle is finished, carefully remove the pan from the bread maker and let it rest.

Remove the bread from the pan, put in a wire rack to Cool about 5 minutes. Slice

# Italian Parmesan Bread

**PREP: 10 MINUTES PLUS FERMENTING TIME /MAKES 1 LOAF**

## Ingredients

- 8 slices bread (1 pound)
- ¾ cup water, at 80°F to 90°F
- 2 tablespoons melted butter, cooled
- 2 teaspoons sugar
- ⅔ teaspoon salt
- 1⅓ teaspoons chopped fresh basil
- 2⅔ tablespoons grated Parmesan cheese
- 2⅓ cups white bread flour
- 1 teaspoon bread machine or instant yeast

## Directions

**1.  Preparing the Ingredients.**

Choose the size of loaf of your preference and then measure the ingredients.

Add all of the ingredients mentioned previously in the list.

Close the lid after placing the pan in the bread machine.

**2.  Select the Bake cycle**

Turn on the bread machine. Select the Quick/Rapid setting, select the loaf size, and the crust color. Press start.

When the cycle is finished, carefully remove the pan from the bread maker and let it rest.

Remove the bread from the pan, put in a wire rack to Cool about 5 minutes. Slice

# Rich Cheddar Bread

**PREP: 10 MINUTES PLUS FERMENTING TIME /MAKES 1 LOAF**

## Ingredients

- 12 slice bread (1½ pounds)
- 1 cup milk, at 80°F to 90°F
- 2 tablespoons butter, melted and cooled
- 3 tablespoons sugar
- 1 teaspoon salt
- ½ cup (2 ounces) grated aged Cheddar cheese
- 3 cups white bread flour
- 2 teaspoons bread machine or instant yeast

## Directions

### 1. Preparing the Ingredients.

Choose the size of loaf of your preference and then measure the ingredients.
Add all of the ingredients mentioned previously in the list.
Close the lid after placing the pan in the bread machine.

### 2. Select the Bake cycle

Turn on the bread machine. Select the Quick/Rapid setting, select the loaf size, and the crust color. Press start.

When the cycle is finished, carefully remove the pan from the bread maker and let it rest.

Remove the bread from the pan, put in a wire rack to Cool about 5 minutes. Slice

# Feta Oregano Bread

**PREP: 10 MINUTES PLUS FERMENTING TIME /MAKES 1 LOAF**

## Ingredients

- 8 slice bread (1 pounds)
- ⅔ cup milk, at 80°F to 90°F
- 2 teaspoons melted butter, cooled
- 2 teaspoons sugar
- ⅔ teaspoon salt
- 2 teaspoons dried oregano
- 2 cups white bread flour
- 1½ teaspoons bread machine or instant yeast
- ⅔ cup (2½ ounces) crumbled feta cheese

## Directions

### 1. Preparing the Ingredients.

Choose the size of loaf of your preference and then measure the ingredients.
Add all of the ingredients mentioned previously in the list.
Close the lid after placing the pan in the bread machine.

**2. Select the Bake cycle**

Turn on the bread machine. Select the Quick/Rapid setting, select the loaf size, and the crust color. Press start.

When the cycle is finished, carefully remove the pan from the bread maker and let it rest.

Remove the bread from the pan, put in a wire rack to Cool about 5 minutes. Slice

# Goat Cheese Bread

**PREP: 10 MINUTES PLUS FERMENTING TIME /MAKES 1 LOAF**

## Ingredients
- 8 slices bread (1 pound)
- ⅔ cup milk, at 80°F to 90°F
- 2⅔ tablespoons goat cheese, at room temperature
- 1 tablespoon honey
- ⅔ teaspoon salt
- ⅔ teaspoon freshly cracked black pepper
- 2 cups white bread flour
- 1 teaspoon bread machine or instant yeast

## Directions
**1. Preparing the Ingredients.**

Choose the size of loaf of your preference and then measure the ingredients.

Add all of the ingredients mentioned previously in the list.

Close the lid after placing the pan in the bread machine.

**2. Select the Bake cycle**

Turn on the bread machine. Select the Quick/Rapid setting, select the loaf size, and the crust color. Press start.

When the cycle is finished, carefully remove the pan from the bread maker and let it rest.

Remove the bread from the pan, put in a wire rack to Cool about 5 minutes. Slice

# Mozzarella-Herb Bread

**PREP: 10 MINUTES PLUS FERMENTING TIME /MAKES 1 LOAF**

## Ingredients
- 12 slice bread (1½ pounds)
- 1¼ cups milk, at 80°F to 90°F
- 1 tablespoon butter, melted and cooled
- 2 tablespoons sugar
- 1 teaspoon salt
- 2 teaspoons dried basil
- 1 teaspoon dried oregano
- 1½ cups (6 ounces) shredded mozzarella cheese
- 3 cups white bread flour
- 2¼ teaspoons bread machine or instant yeast

## Directions
**1. Preparing the Ingredients.**

Choose the size of loaf of your preference and then measure the ingredients.

Add all of the ingredients mentioned previously in the list.

Close the lid after placing the pan in the bread machine.

**2. Select the Bake cycle**

Turn on the bread machine. Select the Quick/Rapid setting, select the loaf size, and the crust color. Press start.

When the cycle is finished, carefully remove the pan from the bread maker and let it rest.

Remove the bread from the pan, put in a wire rack to Cool about 5 minutes. Slice

# Olive Loaf

**PREP: 10 MINUTES PLUS FERMENTING TIME /MAKES 1 LOAF**

## Ingredients

- 1 cup plus 2 tablespoons water
- 1 tablespoon olive oil
- 3 cups bread flour
- 2 tablespoons instant nonfat dry milk
- 1 tablespoon sugar
- 1 1/4 teaspoons salt
- 1/4 teaspoon garlic powder
- 2 teaspoons active dry yeast
- 2/3 cup grated parmesan cheese
- 1 cup pitted Greek olives, sliced and drained

## Directions

**1. Preparing the Ingredients**

Add ingredients, except yeast, olives and cheese, to bread maker in order listed above. Make a well in the flour; pour the yeast into the hole.

**2. Select the Bake cycle**

Select Basic cycle, light crust color, and press Start; do not use delay cycle. Just before the final kneading, add the olives and cheese. Remove and allow to cool on a wire rack for 15 minutes before serving.

# Wine and Cheese Bread

**PREP: 10 MINUTES PLUS FERMENTING TIME /MAKES 1 LOAF**

## Ingredients

- 3/4 cup white wine
- 1/2 cup white cheddar or gruyere cheese, shredded
- 1 1/2 tablespoons butter
- 1/2 teaspoon salt
- 3/4 teaspoon sugar
- 2 1/4 cups bread flour
- 1 1/2 teaspoons active dry yeast

## Directions

1. **Preparing the Ingredients**

Add liquid ingredients to the bread maker pan. Add dry ingredients, except yeast, to the bread pan. Use your fingers to form a well-like hole in the flour where you will pour the yeast; yeast must never come into contact with a liquid when you are adding the ingredients. Carefully pour the yeast into the well.

2. **Select the Bake cycle**

Select Basic bread setting, light crust color, and press Start. Allow to cool on a wire rack before serving.

# SWEET BREAD

## Sugared Doughnuts

**PREP: 30 MINUTES PLUS FERMENTING TIME /MAKES 20 DOUGHNUTS**

**Ingredients**
- 2/3 cup milk
- ¼ cup water
- ¼ cup butter, softened
- 1 egg
- 3 cups bread flour
- ¼ cup sugar
- 1 teaspoon salt
- 2½ teaspoons bread machine or fast-acting dry yeast
- Vegetable oil
- Additional sugar, if desired

**Directions**

1. **Preparing the Ingredients.**

Choose the size of loaf of your preference and then measure the ingredients.

Add all of the ingredients mentioned previously in the list, except for the vegetable oil and additional sugar. Close the lid after placing the pan in the bread machine.

2. **Select the Bake cycle**

Select Dough/Manual cycle. Do not use delay cycle. Remove dough from pan, using lightly floured hands. Cover and let rest 10 minutes on lightly floured board. Roll dough to 3/8-inch thickness on lightly floured board. Cut with floured doughnut cutter. Cover and let rise on board 35 to 45 minutes or until slightly raised.

In deep fryer or heavy Dutch oven, heat 2 to 3 inches oil to 375°F. Fry doughnuts in oil, 2 or 3 at a time, turning as they rise to the surface. Fry 2 to 3 minutes or until golden brown on both sides. Remove from oil with slotted spoon to cooling rack. Roll warm doughnuts in sugar.

## Chocolate Cherry Bread

**PREP: 30 MINUTES PLUS FERMENTING TIME /MAKES 14 SLICES**

**Ingredients**
- 1 cup milk
- 1 egg

- 3 Tbsp water
- 4 tsp butter
- ½ tsp almond extract
- 4 cups bread flour
- 3 Tbsp sugar
- 1 tsp salt
- 1¼ tsp active dry yeast
- ½ cup dried cherries, snipped
- ½ cup semisweet chocolate pieces, chilled

**Directions**

**1. Preparing the Ingredients**

Add each ingredient to the bread machine in the order and at the temperature recommended by your bread machine manufacturer.

**2. Select the Bake cycle**

Close the lid, select the sweet loaf, low crust setting on your bread machine, and press start.

When the bread machine has finished baking, remove the bread and put it on a cooling rack.

# Apple Honey Bread

**PREP: 10 MINUTES PLUS FERMENTING TIME /MAKES 1 LOAF**

**Ingredients**

- 12 slice bread (1½ pounds)
- 5 tablespoons lukewarm milk
- 3 tablespoons apple cider, at room temperature
- 3 tablespoons sugar
- 2 tablespoons unsalted butter, melted
- 1½ tablespoons honey
- ¼ teaspoon table salt
- 3 cups white bread flour
- 1¼ teaspoons bread machine yeast
- 1 apple, peeled, cored, and finely diced

**Directions**

**1. Preparing the Ingredients.**

Choose the size of loaf of your preference and then measure the ingredients.

Add all of the ingredients mentioned previously in the list, except for the apples. Close the lid after placing the pan in the bread machine.

**2. Select the Bake cycle**

Turn on the bread maker. Select the White/Basic or Fruit/Nut (if your machine has this setting) setting, then the loaf size, and finally the crust color. Start the cycle.

When the machine signals to add ingredients, add the apples. When the cycle is finished, carefully remove the pan from the bread maker and let it rest. Remove the bread from the pan, put in a wire rack to Cool about 5 minutes. Slice

# Chocolate Chip Peanut Butter Banana Bread

**PREP: 10 MINUTES PLUS FERMENTING TIME /MAKES 1 LOAF**

**Ingredients**

- 12 to 16 slice bread (1½ to 2 pounds)

- 2 bananas, mashed
- 2 eggs, at room temperature
- ½ cup melted butter, cooled
- 2 tablespoons milk, at room temperature
- 1 teaspoon pure vanilla extract
- 2 cups all-purpose flour
- ½ cup sugar
- 1¼ teaspoons baking powder
- ½ teaspoon baking soda
- ½ teaspoon salt
- ½ cup peanut butter chips
- ½ cup semisweet chocolate chips

**Directions**

1. **Preparing the Ingredients.**
- Stir together the bananas, eggs, butter, milk, and vanilla in the bread machine bucket and set it aside.
- In a medium bowl, toss together the flour, sugar, baking powder, baking soda, salt, peanut butter chips, and chocolate chips.
- Add the dry ingredients to the bucket.
2. **Select the Bake cycle**
- Program the machine for Quick/Rapid bread, and press Start.
- When the loaf is done, stick a knife into it, and if it comes out clean, the loaf is done.
- If the loaf needs a few more minutes, check the control panel for a Bake Only button and extend the time by 10 minutes.
- When the loaf is done, remove the bucket from the machine. Let the loaf cool for 5 minutes.

Gently shake the bucket to remove the loaf, and turn it out onto a rack to cool.

# Easy Apple Coffee Cake

**PREP: 10 MINUTES PLUS FERMENTING TIME /MAKES 10 SERVINGS**

**Ingredients**
- 2⁄3 cup water
- 3 tablespoons butter, softened
- 2 cups bread flour
- 3 tablespoons granulated sugar
- 1 teaspoon salt
- 1½ teaspoons bread machine or fast-acting dry yeast
- 1 cup canned apple pie filling
- Powdered sugar, if desired

**Directions**

1. **Preparing the Ingredients.**

Choose the size of loaf of your preference and then measure the ingredients.

Add all of the ingredients mentioned previously in the list, except for pie filling and powdered sugar.

Close the lid after placing the pan in the bread machine.

Remove dough from pan, using lightly floured hands. Cover and let rest 10 minutes on floured surface.

2. **Select the Bake cycle**

Select Dough/Manual cycle. Do not use delay cycle. Grease large cookie sheet. Roll dough into 13×8-

inch rectangle on lightly floured surface. Place on cookie sheet. Spoon pie filling lengthwise down center third of rectangle. On each 13-inch side, using sharp knife, make cuts from filling to edge of dough at 1-inch intervals. Fold ends up over filling. Fold strips diagonally over filling, alternating sides and overlapping in center. Cover and let rise in warm place 30 to 45 minutes or until doubled in size. Dough is ready if indentation remains when touched. Heat oven to 375°F. Bake 30 to 35 minutes or until golden brown. Remove from cookie sheet to cooling rack; cool. Sprinkle with powdered sugar.

# White Chocolate Bread

**PREP: 10 MINUTES PLUS FERMENTING TIME /MAKES 1 LOAF**

## Ingredients

- 12 slice bread (1½ pounds)
- 1 cup lukewarm milk
- 1 egg, at room temperature
- 2 tablespoons unsalted butter, melted
- 1½ teaspoons pure vanilla extract
- 3 tablespoons light brown sugar
- 4 teaspoons cocoa powder, unsweetened
- ¾ teaspoon table salt
- 3 cups white bread flour
- 1¼ teaspoons bread machine yeast
- ⅓ cup semisweet chocolate chips
- ⅓ cup white chocolate chips

## Directions

**1.    Preparing the Ingredients.**

Choose the size of loaf of your preference and then measure the ingredients.

Add all of the ingredients mentioned previously in the list, except for the the chocolate chips. Close the lid after placing the pan in the bread machine.

**2.  Select the Bake cycle**

Turn on the bread machine. Select the White/Basic or Fruit/Nut (if your machine has this setting) setting, then the loaf size, and finally the crust color. Start the cycle. When the machine signals to add ingredients, add both the chocolate chips. When the cycle is finished, carefully remove the pan from the bread maker and let it rest. Remove the bread from the pan, put in a wire rack to Cool about 5 minutes. Slice

# Chocolate Sour Cream Bread

**PREP: 20 MINUTES PLUS FERMENTING TIME /MAKES 1 LOAF**

## Ingredients

- 12 slice bread (1½ pounds)
- 1 cup sour cream
- 2 eggs, at room temperature
- 1 cup sugar
- ½ cup (1 stick) butter, at room temperature
- ¼ cup plain Greek yogurt
- 1¾ cups all-purpose flour

- ½ cup unsweetened cocoa powder
- ½ teaspoon baking powder
- ½ teaspoon salt
- 1 cup milk chocolate chips

**Directions**

**1. Preparing the Ingredients.**

- In a small bowl, whisk together the sour cream, eggs, sugar, butter, and yogurt until just combined.
- Transfer the wet ingredients to the bread machine bucket, and then add the flour, cocoa powder, baking powder, salt, and chocolate chips. Program the machine for Quick/Rapid bread, and press Start. When the loaf is done, stick a knife into it, and if it comes out clean, the loaf is done.

**2. Select the Bake cycle**

- If the loaf needs a few more minutes, check the control panel for a Bake Only button and extend the time by 10 minutes.
- When the loaf is done, remove the bucket from the machine. Let the loaf cool for 5 minutes. Gently shake the bucket to remove the loaf, and turn it out onto a rack to cool.

# Chocolate Orange Bread

**PREP: 10 MINUTES PLUS FERMENTING TIME /MAKES 14 SLICES**

**Ingredients**

- 1⅝ cups strong white bread flour
- 2 Tbsp cocoa
- 1 tsp ground mixed spice
- 1 egg, beaten
- ½ cup water
- ¼ cup orange juice
- 2 Tbsp butter
- 3 Tbsp light muscovado sugar
- 1 tsp salt
- 1½ tsp easy bake yeast
- ¾ cup mixed peel
- ¾ cup chocolate chips

**Directions**

**1. Preparing the Ingredients**

Sift the flour, cocoa, and spices together in a bowl.

Add each ingredient to the bread machine in the order and at the temperature recommended by your bread machine manufacturer.

**2. Select the Bake cycle**

Close the lid, select the sweet loaf, medium crust setting on your bread machine, and press start.

Add the mixed peel and chocolate chips 5 to 10 minutes before the last kneading cycle ends.

When the bread machine has finished baking, remove the bread and put it on a cooling rack.

# Coffee Cake Banana Bread

**PREP: 10 MINUTES PLUS /MAKES 14 SLICES**

**Ingredients**

- 4 medium bananas, mushed
- 2 Tbsp brown sugar
- 1½ tsp vanilla extract
- ¾ tsp ground cinnamon
- ½ cup butter, softened
- 1 cup sugar
- 2 eggs
- 2 cups all-purpose flour
- 1 tsp baking soda
- ¼ tsp salt
- 2 Tbsp Greek yogurt

**Directions**

**1. Preparing the Ingredients.**

Add each ingredient to the bread machine in the order and at the temperature recommended by your bread machine manufacturer.

**2. Select the Bake cycle**

Close the lid, select the sweet loaf, low crust setting on your bread machine, and press start.

When the bread machine has finished baking, remove the bread and put it on a cooling rack.

# Ginger Spiced Bread

**PREP: 10 MINUTES PLUS FERMENTING TIME /MAKES 1 LOAF**

**Ingredients**

- 12 slice bread (1½ pounds)
- 1 cup lukewarm buttermilk
- 1 egg, at room temperature
- ¼ cup dark molasses
- 1 tablespoon unsalted butter, melted
- 3 tablespoons sugar
- 1½ teaspoons table salt
- 3½ cups white bread flour
- 1 teaspoon ground cinnamon
- ½ teaspoon ground nutmeg
- ¼ teaspoon ground cloves
- 1½ teaspoons ground ginger
- 2 teaspoons bread machine yeast

**Directions**

**1. Preparing the Ingredients.**

Choose the size of loaf of your preference and then measure the ingredients.

Add all of the ingredients mentioned previously in the list.

Close the lid after placing the pan in the bread machine.

**2. Select the Bake cycle**

Turn on the bread machine. Select the Sweet setting, select the loaf size, and the crust color. Press start.

When the cycle is finished, carefully remove the pan from the bread maker and let it rest.

Remove the bread from the pan, put in a wire rack to Cool about 10 minutes. Slice

# Nectarine Cobbler Bread

**PREP: 10 MINUTES PLUS FERMENTING TIME /MAKES 1 LOAF**

**Ingredients**
- 12 to 16 slice bread (1½ to 2 pounds)
- ½ cup (1 stick) butter, at room temperature
- 2 eggs, at room temperature
- 1 cup sugar
- ¼ cup milk, at room temperature
- 1 teaspoon pure vanilla extract
- 1 cup diced nectarines
- 1¾ cups all-purpose flour
- 1 teaspoon baking soda
- ½ teaspoon salt
- ½ teaspoon ground nutmeg
- ¼ teaspoon baking powder

**Directions**

**1.  Preparing the Ingredients.**

Place the butter, eggs, sugar, milk, vanilla, and nectarines in your bread machine.

**2.  Select the Bake cycle**

Program the machine for Quick/Rapid bread and press Start.

While the wet ingredients are mixing, stir together the flour, baking soda, salt, nutmeg, and baking powder in a small bowl.

After the first fast mixing is done and the machine signals, add the dry ingredients.

When the cycle is finished, carefully remove the pan from the bread maker and let it rest.

Remove the bread from the pan, put in a wire rack to Cool about 10 minutes. Slice

# Almond Chocolate Chip Bread

**PREP: 10 MINUTES PLUS FERMENTING TIME /MAKES 14 SLICES**

**Ingredients**
- 1 cup plus 2 Tbsp water
- 2 Tbsp softened butter
- ½ tsp vanilla
- 3 cups Gold Medal Better for Bread flour
- ¾ cup semisweet chocolate chips
- 3 Tbsp sugar
- 1 Tbsp dry milk
- ¾ tsp salt
- 1½ tsp quick active dry yeast
- ⅓ cup sliced almonds

**Directions**

**1.  Preparing the Ingredients**

Add each ingredient except the almonds to the bread machine in the order and at the temperature recommended by your bread machine manufacturer.

**2.  Select the Bake cycle**

Close the lid, select the sweet loaf, low crust setting on your bread machine, and press start.

Add almonds 10 minutes before last kneading cycle ends. When the bread machine has finished baking, remove the bread and put it on a cooling rack.

# Swedish Coffee Bread

**PREP: 10 MINUTES /MAKES 14 SLICES**

**Ingredients**
- 1 cup milk
- ½ tsp salt
- 1 egg yolk
- 2 Tbsp softened butter
- 3 cups all-purpose flour
- ⅓ cup sugar
- 1 envelope active dry yeast
- 3 tsp ground cardamom
- 2 egg whites, slightly beaten

**Directions**

**1. Preparing the Ingredients**

Add each ingredient to the bread machine in the order and at the temperature recommended by your bread machine manufacturer.

**2. Select the Bake cycle**

Select the dough cycle and press start. Grease your baking sheet.

When the dough cycle has finished, divide the dough into three equal parts. Roll each part into a rope 12-14" long. Lay 3 ropes side by side, and then braid them together.

Tuck the ends underneath and put onto the sheet. Next, cover the bread, using kitchen towel, and let it rise until it has doubled in size. Brush your bread with beaten egg white and sprinkle with pearl sugar. Bake until golden brown at 375˚F in a preheated oven for 20-25 minutes. When baked, remove the bread and put it on a cooling rack.

# Pear Kuchen with Ginger Topping

**PREP: 20 MINUTES PLUS FERMENTING TIME /MAKES 12 SERVINGS**

**Ingredients**

**Bread dough**
- ½ cup milk
- 2 tablespoons butter, softened
- 1 egg
- 2 cups bread flour
- 2 tablespoons sugar
- 1 teaspoon salt
- 1¾ teaspoons bread machine or fast-acting dry yeast

**Topping**
- 3 cups sliced peeled pears
- 1 cup sugar
- 2 tablespoons butter, softened

- 1 tablespoon chopped crystallized ginger
- ½ cup whipping cream
- 1 egg yolk

**Directions**

**1.  Preparing the Ingredients.**

Measure carefully, placing all bread dough ingredients in bread machine pan in the order recommended by the manufacturer.

**2.  Select the Bake cycle**

Select Dough/Manual cycle. Do not use delay cycle.

Remove dough from pan, using lightly floured hands. Cover and let rest 10 minutes on lightly floured surface.

Grease 13×9-inch pan with shortening. Press dough evenly in bottom of pan.

Arrange pears on dough. In small bowl, mix 1 cup sugar, 2 tablespoons butter and the ginger. Reserve 2 tablespoons of the topping; sprinkle remaining topping over pears. Cover and let rise in warm place 30 to 45 minutes or until doubled in size. Dough is ready if indentation remains when touched.

Heat oven to 375°F. Bake 20 minutes. Mix whipping cream and egg yolk; pour over hot kuchen. Bake 15 minutes longer or until golden brown. Sprinkle with reserved 2 tablespoons topping. Serve warm.

# Walnut Cocoa Bread

**PREP: 20 MINUTES PLUS FERMENTING TIME /MAKES 14 SERVINGS**

**Ingredients**

- ⅔ cup milk
- ⅓ cup water
- 5 Tbsp butter, softened
- ⅓ cup packed brown sugar
- 5 Tbsp baking cocoa
- 1 tsp salt
- 3 cups bread flour
- 2¼ tsp active dry yeast
- ⅔ cup chopped walnuts, toasted

**Directions**

**1.  Preparing the Ingredients**

Add each ingredient except the walnuts to the bread machine in the order and at the temperature recommended by your bread machine manufacturer.

**2.  Select the Bake cycle**

Close the lid, select the sweet loaf, low crust setting on your bread machine, and press start.

Just before the final kneading, add the walnuts.

When the bread machine has finished baking, remove the bread and put it on a cooling rack.

# Sweet Applesauce Bread

**PREP: 10 MINUTES PLUS FERMENTING TIME /MAKES 1 LOAF**

**Ingredients**

- 12 slice bread (1½ pounds)
- ⅔ cup lukewarm milk

- ¼ cup unsweetened applesauce, at room temperature
- 1 tablespoon unsalted butter, melted
- 1 tablespoon sugar
- 1 teaspoon table salt
- ¼ cup quick oats
- 2¼ cups white bread flour
- ½ teaspoon ground cinnamon
- Pinch ground nutmeg
- 2¼ teaspoons bread machine yeast

## Directions

### 1. Preparing the Ingredients .

Choose the size of loaf of your preference and then measure the ingredients.

Add all of the ingredients mentioned previously in the list.

Close the lid after placing the pan in the bread machine.

### 2. Select the Bake cycle

Turn on the bread machine. Select the Quick/Rapid setting, select the loaf size, and the crust color. Press start.

When the cycle is finished, carefully remove the pan from the bread maker and let it rest.

Remove the bread from the pan, put in a wire rack to Cool about 5 minutes. Slice

# Mexican Chocolate Bread

**PREP: 10 MINUTES PLUS FERMENTING TIME /MAKES 1 LOAF**

## Ingredients

- ½ cup milk
- ½ cup orange juice
- 1 large egg plus 1 egg yolk
- 3 Tbsp unsalted butter cut into pieces
- 2½ cups bread flour
- ¼ cup light brown sugar
- 3 Tbsp unsweetened dutch-process cocoa powder
- 1 Tbsp gluten
- 1 tsp instant espresso powder
- ¾ tsp ground cinnamon
- ½ cup bittersweet chocolate chips
- 2½ tsp bread machine yeast

## Directions

### 1. Preparing the Ingredients.

Add each ingredient to the bread machine in the order and at the temperature recommended by your bread machine manufacturer.

### 2. Select the Bake cycle

Close the lid, select the sweet loaf, low crust setting on your bread machine, and press start.

When the bread machine has finished baking, remove the bread and put it on a cooling rack.

# Sour Cream Maple Bread

**PREP: 10 MINUTES PLUS FERMENTING TIME /MAKES 1 LOAF**

**Ingredients**
- 8 slices bread (1 pound)
- 6 tablespoons water, at 80°F to 90°F
- 6 tablespoons sour cream, at room temperature
- 1½ tablespoons butter, at room temperature
- ¾ tablespoon maple syrup
- ½ teaspoon salt
- 1¾ cups white bread flour
- 1⅛ teaspoons bread machine or instant yeast

**Directions**
**1.  Preparing the Ingredients.**
Choose the size of loaf of your preference and then measure the ingredients.
Add all of the ingredients mentioned previously in the list.
Close the lid after placing the pan in the bread machine.
**2.  Select the Bake cycle**
Turn on the bread machine. Select the Quick/Rapid setting, select the loaf size, and the crust color. Press start.
When the cycle is finished, carefully remove the pan from the bread maker and let it rest.

Remove the bread from the pan, put in a wire rack to Cool about 5 minutes. Slice

# Chocolate Chip Bread

**PREP: 10 MINUTES PLUS FERMENTING TIME /MAKES 1 LOAF**

**Ingredients**
- ¼ cup water
- 1 cup milk
- 1 egg
- 3 cups bread flour
- 3 Tbsp brown sugar
- 2 Tbsp white sugar
- 1 tsp salt
- 1 tsp ground cinnamon
- 1½ tsp active dry yeast
- 2 Tbsp margarine, softened
- ¾ cup semisweet chocolate chips

**Directions**
**1.  Preparing the Ingredients**
Add each ingredient except the chocolate chips to the bread machine in the order and at the temperature recommended by your bread machine manufacturer.
**2.  Select the Bake cycle**
Close the lid, select the sweet loaf, low crust setting on your bread machine, and press start.
Add the chocolate chips about 5 minutes before the kneading cycle has finished. When the bread

machine has finished baking, remove the bread and put it on a cooling rack .

# Crunchy Wheat-and-Honey Twist
### PREP: 10 MINUTES PLUS FERMENTING TIME /MAKES 1 LOAF

**Ingredients**
* 16 slice bread (2 pounds)
* Bread dough
* ¾ cup plus 2 tablespoons water
* 2 tablespoons honey
* 1 tablespoon butter, softened
* 1¼ cups whole wheat flour
* 1 cup bread flour
* 1/3 cup slivered almonds, toasted
* 1 teaspoon salt
* 1 teaspoon bread machine or fast-acting dry yeast
* Topping
* Butter, melted
* 1 egg, slightly beaten
* 2 tablespoons sugar
* ¼ teaspoon ground cinnamon

**Directions**

**1. Preparing the Ingredients.**

Measure carefully, placing all bread dough ingredients in bread machine pan in the order recommended by the manufacturer.

Select Dough/Manual cycle. Do not use delay cycle.

Remove dough from pan, using lightly floured hands. Cover and let rest 10 minutes on lightly floured surface.

Grease large cookie sheet with shortening. Divide dough in half. Roll each half into 15-inch rope. Place ropes side by side on cookie sheet; twist together gently and loosely. Pinch ends to seal. Brush melted butter lightly over dough.

**2. Select the Bake cycle**

Cover and let rise in warm place 45 to 60 minutes or until doubled in size.

Dough is ready if indentation remains when touched.

Heat oven to 375°F. Brush egg over dough. Mix sugar and cinnamon; sprinkle over dough. Bake 25 to 30 minutes or until twist is golden brown and sounds hollow when tapped. Remove from cookie sheet to cooling rack; cool 20 minutes.

To toast almonds, bake in ungreased shallow pan at 350°F for 6 to 10 minutes, stirring occasionally, until light brown.

# Milk Sweet Bread
### PREP: 10 MINUTES PLUS FERMENTING TIME /MAKES 1 LOAF

**Ingredients**
* 12 slice bread (1½ pounds)
* 1 cup lukewarm milk
* 1 egg, at room temperature

- 2 tablespoons butter, softened
- ½ cup sugar
- 1 teaspoon table salt
- 3 cups white bread flour
- 2¼ teaspoons bread machine yeast

**Directions**
**1. Preparing the Ingredients.**
Choose the size of loaf of your preference and then measure the ingredients.
Add all of the ingredients mentioned previously in the list.
Close the lid after placing the pan in the bread machine.
**2. Select the Bake cycle**
Turn on the bread machine. Select the Sweet setting, select the loaf size, and the crust color. Press start.
When the cycle is finished, carefully remove the pan from the bread maker and let it rest.

Remove the bread from the pan, put in a wire rack to Cool about 5 minutes. Slice

# Barmbrack Bread

**PREP: 10 MINUTES PLUS FERMENTING TIME /MAKES 1 LOAF**

**Ingredients**
- 8 slices bread (1 pound)
- ⅔ cup water, at 80°F to 90°F
- 1 tablespoon melted butter, cooled
- 2 tablespoons sugar
- 2 tablespoons skim milk powder
- 1 teaspoon salt
- 1 teaspoon dried lemon zest
- ¼ teaspoon ground allspice
- ⅛ teaspoon ground nutmeg
- 2 cups white bread flour
- 1½ teaspoons bread machine or active dry yeast
- ½ cup dried currants

**Directions**
**1. Preparing the Ingredients.**
Place the ingredients, except the currants, in your bread machine as recommended by the manufacturer.
**2. Select the Bake cycle**
Program the machine for Basic/White bread, select light or medium crust, and press Start.
Add the currants when your machine signals or when the second kneading cycle starts. When the cycle
is finished, carefully remove the pan from the bread maker and let it rest. Remove the bread from the
pan, put in a wire rack to Cool about 5 minutes. Slice

# Pumpernickel Bread

**PREP: 10 MINUTES PLUS FERMENTING TIME /MAKES 12 SLICES**

**Ingredients**

- 1 cup plus 2 tablespoons water
- 1½ teaspoons salt
- 1/3 cup molasses
- 2 tablespoons vegetable oil
- 1 cup plus 1 tablespoon rye flour
- 1 cup plus 2 tablespoons whole wheat flour
- 1½ cups bread flour
- 3 tablespoons unsweetened baking cocoa
- 1½ teaspoons instant coffee granules or crystals
- 1 tablespoon caraway seed
- 1 teaspoon bread machine or fast-acting dry yeast

## Directions
### 1. Preparing the Ingredients.
Measure carefully, placing all ingredients in bread machine pan in the order recommended by the manufacturer.
### 2. Select the Bake cycle
Select Whole Wheat or Basic/White cycle. Use Medium or Light crust color.
Remove baked bread from pan; cool on cooling rack.

# Allspice Currant Bread
**PREP: 10 MINUTES PLUS FERMENTING TIME /MAKES 1 LOAF**

## Ingredients
- 16 slice bread (2 pounds)
- 1½ cups lukewarm water
- 2 tablespoons unsalted butter, melted
- ¼ cup sugar
- ¼ cup skim milk powder
- 2 teaspoons table salt
- 4 cups white bread flour
- 1½ teaspoons dried lemon zest
- ¾ teaspoon ground allspice
- ¼ teaspoon ground nutmeg
- 2½ teaspoons bread machine yeast
- 1 cup dried currants

## Directions
### 1. Preparing the Ingredients.
Choose the size of loaf of your preference and then measure the ingredients.
Add all of the ingredients mentioned previously in the list, except for the dried currants. Close the lid after placing the pan in the bread machine.
### 2. Select the Bake cycle
Turn on the bread maker. Select the White/Basic or Fruit/Nut (if your machine has this setting) setting, then the loaf size, and finally the crust color. Start the cycle.
When the machine signals to add ingredients, add the dried currants.
When the cycle is finished, carefully remove the pan from the bread maker and let it rest. Remove the

bread from the pan, put in a wire rack to Cool about 5 minutes. Slice

# Apple Butter Bread

**PREP: 10 MINUTES PLUS FERMENTING TIME /MAKES 1 LOAF**

**Ingredients**
- 8 slices bread (1 pound)
- ⅔ cup milk, at 80°F to 90°F
- ⅓ cup apple butter, at room temperature
- 4 teaspoons melted butter, cooled
- 2 teaspoons honey
- ⅔ teaspoon salt
- ⅔ cup whole-wheat flour
- 1½ cups white bread flour
- 1 teaspoon bread machine or instant yeast

**Directions**
**1. Preparing the Ingredients.**
Choose the size of loaf of your preference and then measure the ingredients.
Add all of the ingredients mentioned previously in the list.
Close the lid after placing the pan in the bread machine.
**2. Select the Bake cycle**
Turn on the bread machine. Select the Quick/Rapid setting, select the loaf size, and the crust color. Press start.
When the cycle is finished, carefully remove the pan from the bread maker and let it rest.

Remove the bread from the pan, put in a wire rack to Cool about 5 minutes. Slice

# Beer and Pretzel Bread

**PREP: 10 MINUTES PLUS FERMENTING TIME /MAKES 12 SLICES**

**Ingredients**
- ¾ cup regular or nonalcoholic beer
- 1/3 cup water
- 2 tablespoons butter, softened
- 3 cups bread flour
- 1 tablespoon packed brown sugar
- 1 teaspoon ground mustard
- 1 teaspoon salt
- 1½ teaspoons bread machine yeast
- ½ cup bite-size pretzel pieces, about 1×¾ inch, or pretzel rods, cut into 1-inch pieces

**Directions**
**1. Preparing the Ingredients.**
Measure carefully, placing all ingredients except pretzels in bread machine pan in order recommended by the manufacturer.
**2. Select the Bake cycle**
Select Basic/White cycle. Use Medium or Light crust color. Do not use delay cycle.
Add pretzels 5 minutes before the last kneading cycle ends. Remove baked bread from pan; cool on

cooling rack.

# Buttermilk Pecan Bread

**PREP: 10 MINUTES PLUS FERMENTING TIME /MAKES 1 LOAF**

## Ingredients
- 12 slice bread (1½ pounds)
- ¾ cup buttermilk, at room temperature
- ¾ cup butter, at room temperature
- 1 tablespoon instant coffee granules
- 3 eggs, at room temperature
- ¾ cup sugar
- 2 cups all-purpose flour
- ½ tablespoon baking powder
- ½ teaspoon table salt
- 1 cup chopped pecans

## Directions
**1. Preparing the Ingredients.**
Choose the size of loaf of your preference and then measure the ingredients.
Add all of the ingredients mentioned previously in the list.
Close the lid after placing the pan in the bread machine.
**2. Select the Bake cycle**
Turn on the bread machine. Select the Quick/Rapid setting, select the loaf size, and the crust color. Press start.
When the cycle is finished, carefully remove the pan from the bread maker and let it rest.

Remove the bread from the pan, put in a wire rack to Cool about 5 minutes. Slice

# Crusty Honey Bread

**PREP: 10 MINUTES PLUS FERMENTING TIME /MAKES 1 LOAF**

## Ingredients
- 12 slice bread (1½ pounds)
- 1 cup minus 1 tablespoon water, at 80°F to 90°F
- 1½ tablespoons honey
- 1⅛ tablespoons melted butter, cooled
- ¾ teaspoon salt
- 2⅔ cups white bread flour
- 1½ teaspoons bread machine or instant yeast

## Directions
**1. Preparing the Ingredients.**
Choose the size of loaf of your preference and then measure the ingredients.
Add all of the ingredients mentioned previously in the list.
Close the lid after placing the pan in the bread machine.
**2. Select the Bake cycle**
Turn on the bread machine. Select the Basic/White setting, select the loaf size, and the crust color. Press

start.

When the cycle is finished, carefully remove the pan from the bread maker and let it rest.

Remove the bread from the pan, put in a wire rack to Cool about 5 minutes. Slice

# Brown Sugar Date Nut Swirl Bread

**PREP: 10 MINUTES PLUS FERMENTING TIME /MAKES 1 LOAF**

**Ingredients**
- 1 cup milk
- 1 large egg
- 4 tablespoons butter
- 4 tablespoons sugar
- 1 teaspoon salt
- 4 cups flour
- 1 2/3 teaspoons yeast
- For the filling:
- 1/2 cup packed brown sugar
- 1 cup walnuts, chopped
- 1 cup medjool dates, pitted and chopped
- 2 teaspoons cinnamon
- 2 teaspoons clove spice
- 1 1/3 tablespoons butter
- Powdered sugar, sifted

**Directions**

**1. Preparing the Ingredients**

Add wet ingredients to the bread maker pan. Mix flour, sugar and salt and add to pan.
Make a well in the center of the dry ingredients and add the yeast.

**2. Select the Bake cycle**

Select the Dough cycle and press Start. Punch the dough down and allow it to rest in a warm place. Mix the brown sugar with walnuts, dates and spices; set aside. Roll the dough into a rectangle, on a lightly floured surface. Baste with a tablespoon of butter, add the filling. Start from the short side and roll the dough to form a jelly roll shape. Place the roll into a greased loaf pan and cover. Let it rise in a warm place, until nearly doubled in size; about 30 minutes. Bake at 350°F for approximately 30 minutes. Cover with foil during the last 10 minutes of cooking.
Transfer to a cooling rack for 15 minutes; sprinkle with the powdered sugar and serve.

# Cashew Butter/Peanut Butter Bread

**PREP: 10 MINUTES PLUS FERMENTING TIME /MAKES 1 LOAF**

**Ingredients**
- 12 slice bread (1½ pounds)
- 1 cup peanut butter or cashew butter
- 1 cup lukewarm milk
- ½ cup packed light brown sugar
- ¼ cup sugar
- ¼ cup butter, at room temperature

- 1 egg, at room temperature
- 2 teaspoons pure vanilla extract
- 2 cups all-purpose flour
- 1 tablespoon baking powder
- ½ teaspoon table salt

**Directions**

**1. Preparing the Ingredients.**

Choose the size of loaf of your preference and then measure the ingredients. Add all of the ingredients mentioned previously in the list. Close the lid after placing the pan in the bread machine.

**2. Select the Bake cycle**

Turn on the bread machine. Select the Quick/Rapid setting, select the loaf size, and the crust color. Press start.

When the cycle is finished, carefully remove the pan from the bread maker and let it rest.

Remove the bread from the pan, put in a wire rack to Cool about 5 minutes. Slice

# Honey Granola Bread

**PREP: 10 MINUTES PLUS FERMENTING TIME /MAKES 1 LOAF**

**Ingredients**

- 12 slice bread (1½ pounds)
- 1⅛ cups milk, at 80°F to 90°F
- 3 tablespoons honey
- 1½ tablespoons butter, melted and cooled
- 1⅛ teaspoons salt
- ¾ cup whole-wheat flour
- ⅔ cup prepared granola, crushed
- 1¾ cups white bread flour
- 1½ teaspoons bread machine or instant yeast

**Directions**

**1. Preparing the Ingredients.**

Choose the size of loaf of your preference and then measure the ingredients.
Add all of the ingredients mentioned previously in the list.
Close the lid after placing the pan in the bread machine.

**2. Select the Bake cycle**

Turn on the bread machine. Select the Basic/White setting, select the loaf size, and the crust color. Press start.

When the cycle is finished, carefully remove the pan from the bread maker and let it rest.

Remove the bread from the pan, put in a wire rack to Cool about 5 minutes. Slice

# Delicious Sour Cream Bread

**PREP: 10 MINUTES PLUS FERMENTING TIME /MAKES 1 LOAF**

**Ingredients**

- 12 slice bread (1½ pounds)

- ½ cup + 1 tablespoon lukewarm water
- ½ cup + 1 tablespoon sour cream, at room temperature
- 2¼ tablespoons butter, at room temperature
- 1 tablespoon maple syrup
- ¾ teaspoon table salt
- 2¾ cups white bread flour
- 1⅔ teaspoons bread machine yeast

**Directions**

**1. Preparing the Ingredients.**

Choose the size of loaf of your preference and then measure the ingredients.

Add all of the ingredients mentioned previously in the list.

Close the lid after placing the pan in the bread machine.

**2. Select the Bake cycle**

Turn on the bread machine. Select the Basic/White setting, select the loaf size, and the crust color. Press start.

When the cycle is finished, carefully remove the pan from the bread maker and let it rest.

Remove the bread from the pan, put in a wire rack to Cool about 5 minutes. Slice

# Black Bread

**PREP: 10 MINUTES PLUS FERMENTING TIME /MAKES 1 LOAF**

**Ingredients**

- 12 slice bread (1½ pounds)
- ¾ cup water, at 80°F to 90°F
- ⅓ cup brewed coffee, at 80°F to 90°F
- 1½ tablespoons balsamic vinegar
- 1½ tablespoons olive oil
- 1½ tablespoons dark molasses
- ¾ tablespoon light brown sugar
- ¾ teaspoon salt
- 1½ teaspoons caraway seeds
- 3 tablespoons unsweetened cocoa powder
- ¾ cup dark rye flour
- 1¾ cups white bread flour
- 1½ teaspoons bread machine or instant yeast

**Directions**

**1. Preparing the Ingredients.**

Place the ingredients in your bread machine as recommended by the manufacturer.

**2. Select the Bake cycle**

Program the machine for Whole-Wheat/Whole-Grain bread, select light or medium crust, and press Start.

When the loaf is done, remove the bucket from the machine. Let the loaf cool for 5 minutes. Gently shake the bucket to remove the loaf, and turn it out onto a rack to cool.

# Cinnamon Bread

**PREP: 10 MINUTES PLUS FERMENTING TIME /MAKES 1 LOAF**

## Ingredients

- 12 slice bread (1½ pounds)
- ¾ cup lukewarm water
- 1 egg, at room temperature
- 3 tablespoons butter, melted and cooled
- 3 tablespoons sugar
- 1 tablespoon rum extract
- 1¼ teaspoons table salt
- 3 cups white bread flour
- 1 teaspoon ground cinnamon
- ¼ teaspoon ground nutmeg
- 1 teaspoon bread machine yeast

## Directions

### 1. Preparing the Ingredients.

Choose the size of loaf of your preference and then measure the ingredients.

Add all of the ingredients mentioned previously in the list.

Close the lid after placing the pan in the bread machine.

### 2. Select the Bake cycle

Turn on the bread machine. Select the Basic/White setting, select the loaf size, and the crust color. Press start.

When the cycle is finished, carefully remove the pan from the bread maker and let it rest.

Remove the bread from the pan, put in a wire rack to Cool about 5 minutes. Slice

# Apple Cider Bread

**PREP: 10 MINUTES PLUS FERMENTING TIME /MAKES 1 LOAF**

## Ingredients

- 8 slices bread (1 pound)
- ¼ cup milk, at 80°F to 90°F
- 2 tablespoons apple cider, at room temperature
- 2 tablespoons sugar
- 4 teaspoons melted butter, cooled
- 1 tablespoon honey
- ¼ teaspoon salt
- 2 cups white bread flour
- ¾ teaspoons bread machine or instant yeast
- ⅔ apple, peeled, cored, and finely diced

## Directions

### 1. Preparing the Ingredients.

Place the ingredients, except the apple, in your bread machine as recommended by the manufacturer.

### 2. Select the Bake cycle

Program the machine for Basic/White bread, select light or medium crust, and press Start.

Add the apple when the machine signals or 5 minutes before the last kneading cycle is complete.
When the cycle is finished, carefully remove the pan from the bread maker and let it rest.
Remove the bread from the pan, put in a wire rack to Cool about 5 minutes. Slice

# Sweet Pineapple Bread

**PREP: 10 MINUTES PLUS FERMENTING TIME /MAKES 1 LOAF**

## Ingredients
- 16 slice bread (2 pounds)
- 6 tablespoons unsalted butter, melted
- 2 eggs, at room temperature
- ½ cup coconut milk, at room temperature
- ½ cup pineapple juice, at room temperature
- 1 cup sugar
- 1½ teaspoons coconut extract
- 2 cups all-purpose flour
- ¾ cup shredded sweetened coconut
- 1 teaspoon baking powder
- ½ teaspoon table salt

## Directions
**1. Preparing the Ingredients.**
Place the ingredients, except the apple, in your bread machine as recommended by the manufacturer.
**2. Select the Bake cycle**
Program the machine for Quick/Rapid bread, select light or medium crust, and press Start.
Add the apple when the machine signals or 5 minutes before the last kneading cycle is complete.
When the cycle is finished, carefully remove the pan from the bread maker and let it rest.
Remove the bread from the pan, put in a wire rack to Cool about 5 minutes. Slice

# Coffee Cake

**PREP: 10 MINUTES PLUS FERMENTING TIME /MAKES 1 LOAF**

## Ingredients
- 12 to 16 slice bread (1½ to 2 pounds)
- ¾ cup buttermilk, at room temperature
- ¾ cup (1½ sticks) butter, at room temperature
- 1 tablespoon instant coffee granules
- 3 eggs, at room temperature
- ¾ cup sugar
- 2 cups all-purpose flour
- ½ tablespoon baking powder
- ½ teaspoon salt
- 1 cup chopped pecans

## Directions
**1. Preparing the Ingredients.**
Place the buttermilk, butter, coffee granules, eggs, and sugar in the bread maker.

**2. Select the Bake cycle**

Program the machine for Quick/Rapid bread and press Start. While the wet ingredients are mixing, stir together the flour, baking powder, salt, and pecans in a small bowl. After the first fast mixing is done and the machine signals, add the dry ingredients. When the cycle is finished, carefully remove the pan from the bread maker and let it rest.

Remove the bread from the pan, put in a wire rack to Cool about 5 minutes. Slice

# Caramel Apple and Pecan Bread

**PREP: 10 MINUTES PLUS FERMENTING TIME /MAKES 1 LOAF**

**Ingredients**

- 12 slice bread (1½ pounds)
- 1 cup water
- 2 tablespoons butter, softened
- 3 cups bread flour
- ¼ cup packed brown sugar
- ¾ teaspoon ground cinnamon
- 1 teaspoon salt
- 2 teaspoons bread machine or fast-acting dry yeast
- ½ cup chopped unpeeled apple
- 1/3 cup coarsely chopped pecans, toasted

**Directions**

**1. Preparing the Ingredients.**

Choose the size of loaf of your preference and then measure the ingredients.

Add all of the ingredients mentioned previously in the list except apple and pecans in bread maker. Add apple and pecans at the Raisin/Nut signal or 5 to 10 minutes before last kneading cycle ends.

**2. Select the Bake cycle**

Program the machine for Basic/White bread and press Start.

When the cycle is finished, carefully remove the pan from the bread maker and let it rest.

Remove the bread from the pan, put in a wire rack to Cool about 5 minutes. Slice

# Cocoa Banana Bread

**PREP: 10 MINUTES PLUS FERMENTING TIME /MAKES 1 LOAF**

**Ingredients**

- 12 slice bread (1½ pounds)
- 3 bananas, mashed
- 2 eggs, at room temperature
- ¾ cup packed light brown sugar
- ½ cup unsalted butter, melted
- ½ cup sour cream, at room temperature
- ¼ cup sugar
- 1½ teaspoons pure vanilla extract
- 1 cup all-purpose flour
- ½ cup quick oats
- 2 tablespoons unsweetened cocoa powder
- 1 teaspoon baking soda

**Directions**

**1. Preparing the Ingredients.**

Choose the size of loaf of your preference and then measure the ingredients.

Add all of the ingredients mentioned previously in the list.

Close the lid after placing the pan in the bread machine.

**2. Select the Bake cycle**

Turn on the bread machine. Select the Quick/Rapid setting, select the loaf size, and the crust color. Press start.

When the cycle is finished, carefully remove the pan from the bread maker and let it rest.

Remove the bread from the pan, put in a wire rack to Cool about 5 minutes. Slice

# Pumpkin Coconut Bread

**PREP: 10 MINUTES PLUS FERMENTING TIME /MAKES 1 LOAF**

**Ingredients**

- 12 to 16 slice bread (1½ to 2 pounds)
- 1 cup pure canned pumpkin
- ½ cup (1 stick) butter, at room temperature
- 1½ teaspoons pure vanilla extract
- 1 cup sugar
- ½ cup dark brown sugar
- 2 cups all-purpose flour
- ¾ cup sweetened shredded coconut
- 1½ teaspoons ground cinnamon
- 1 teaspoon baking soda
- 1 teaspoon baking powder
- ½ teaspoon ground nutmeg
- ½ teaspoon ground ginger
- ⅛ teaspoon ground allspice

**Directions**

**1. Preparing the Ingredients.**

Place the pumpkin, butter, vanilla, sugar, and dark brown sugar in your bread machine.

**2. Select the Bake cycle**

Program the machine for Quick/Rapid bread and press Start.

After the first fast mixing is done, add the flour, coconut, cinnamon, baking soda, baking powder, nutmeg, ginger, and allspice.

When the cycle is finished, carefully remove the pan from the bread maker and let it rest.

Remove the bread from the pan, put in a wire rack to Cool about 5 minutes. Slice.

# Cranberry-Cornmeal Bread

**PREP: 10 MINUTES PLUS FERMENTING TIME /MAKES 1 LOAF**

**Ingredients**

- 12 slice bread (1½ pounds)
- 1 cup plus 1 tablespoon water
- 3 tablespoons molasses or honey
- 2 tablespoons butter, softened

- 3 cups bread flour
- 1/3 cup cornmeal
- 1½ teaspoons salt
- 2 teaspoons bread machine yeast
- ½ cup sweetened dried cranberries

**Directions**

**1. Preparing the Ingredients.**

Choose the size of loaf of your preference and then measure the ingredients.

Add all of the ingredients mentioned previously in the list except cranberries

Close the lid after placing the pan in the bread machine.

Add cranberries at the Raisin/Nut signal or 5 to 10 minutes before last kneading cycle ends.

**2. Select the Bake cycle**

Program the machine for White/Basic bread and press Start.

After the first fast mixing is done, add the flour, coconut, cinnamon, baking soda, baking powder, nutmeg, ginger, and allspice. When the cycle is finished, carefully remove the pan from the bread maker and let it rest.

Remove the bread from the pan, put in a wire rack to Cool about 5 minutes. Slice.

# Coconut Delight Bread

**PREP: 10 MINUTES PLUS FERMENTING TIME /MAKES 1 LOAF**

**Ingredients**

- 16 slice bread (2 pounds)
- 1⅓ cups lukewarm milk
- 1 egg, at room temperature
- 2 tablespoons unsalted butter, melted
- 2⅔ teaspoons pure coconut extract
- 3⅓ tablespoons sugar
- 1 teaspoon table salt
- ⅔ cup sweetened shredded coconut
- 4 cups white bread flour
- 2 teaspoons bread machine yeast

**Directions**

**1. Preparing the Ingredients.**

Choose the size of loaf of your preference and then measure the ingredients.

Add all of the ingredients mentioned previously in the list.

Close the lid after placing the pan in the bread machine.

**2. Select the Bake cycle**

Turn on the bread machine. Select the Sweet setting, select the loaf size, and the crust color. Press start.

When the cycle is finished, carefully remove the pan from the bread maker and let it rest.

Remove the bread from the pan, put in a wire rack to Cool about 5 minutes. Slice

# Vanilla Almond Milk Bread

**PREP: 10 MINUTES PLUS FERMENTING TIME /MAKES 1 LOAF**

**Ingredients**

- 12 slice bread (1½ pounds)
- ½ cup plus 1 tablespoon milk, at 80°F to 90°F
- 3 tablespoons melted butter, cooled
- 3 tablespoons sugar
- 1 egg, at room temperature
- 1½ teaspoons pure vanilla extract
- ⅓ teaspoon almond extract
- 2½ cups white bread flour
- 1½ teaspoons bread machine or instant yeast

**Directions**

**1. Preparing the Ingredients.**

Choose the size of loaf of your preference and then measure the ingredients.

Add all of the ingredients mentioned previously in the list.

Close the lid after placing the pan in the bread machine.

**2. Select the Bake cycle**

Turn on the bread machine. Select the Sweet setting, select the loaf size, and the crust color. Press start.

When the cycle is finished, carefully remove the pan from the bread maker and let it rest.

Remove the bread from the pan, put in a wire rack to Cool about 5 minutes. Slice

# Hot Cross Buns

**PREP: 10 MINUTES PLUS FERMENTING TIME /MAKES 16 BOUNS**

**Ingredients**

**Dough**

- 2 eggs plus enough water to equal 11/3 cups
- ½ cup butter, softened
- 4 cups bread flour
- ¾ teaspoon ground cinnamon
- ¼ teaspoon ground nutmeg
- 1½ teaspoons salt
- 2 tablespoons granulated sugar
- 1½ teaspoons bread machine or fast-acting dry yeast
- ½ cup raisins
- ½ cup golden raisins
- 1 egg
- 2 tablespoons cold water

**Icing**

- 1 cup powdered sugar
- 1 tablespoon milk or water
- ½ teaspoon vanilla

**Directions**

**1. Preparing the Ingredients.**

Measure carefully, placing all dough ingredients except raisins, 1 egg and the cold water in bread machine pan in the order recommended by the manufacturer. Add raisins at the Raisin/Nut signal.

**2. Select the Bake cycle**

Select Dough/Manual cycle. Do not use delay cycle. Remove dough from pan, using lightly floured hands. Cover and let rest 10 minutes on lightly floured surface. Grease cookie sheet or 2 (9-inch) round pans. Divide dough in half. Divide each half into 8 equal pieces. Shape each piece into a smooth ball. Place balls about 2 inches apart on cookie sheet or 1 inch apart in pans. Using scissors, snip a cross shape in top of each ball. Cover and let rise in warm place about 40 minutes or until doubled in size. Heat oven to 375°F. Beat egg and cold water slightly; brush on buns. Bake 18 to 20 minutes or until golden brown. Remove from cookie sheet to cooling rack. Cool slightly.

In small bowl, mix all icing ingredients until smooth and spreadable. Make a cross on top of each bun with icing.

# Chocolate Chip Bread

**PREP: 10 MINUTES PLUS FERMENTING TIME /MAKES 1 LOAF**

## Ingredients

- 12 slice bread (1½ pounds)
- 1 cup sour cream
- 2 eggs, at room temperature
- 1 cup sugar
- ½ cup unsalted butter, melted
- ¼ cup plain Greek yogurt
- 1¾ cups all-purpose flour
- ½ cup unsweetened cocoa powder
- ½ teaspoon baking powder
- ½ teaspoon table salt
- 1 cup milk chocolate chips

## Directions

**1. Preparing the Ingredients.**

Choose the size of loaf of your preference and then measure the ingredients.

Add all of the ingredients mentioned previously in the list.

Close the lid after placing the pan in the bread machine.

**2. Select the Bake cycle**

Turn on the bread machine. Select the Quick/Rapid setting, select the loaf size, and the crust color. Press start.

When the cycle is finished, carefully remove the pan from the bread maker and let it rest.

Remove the bread from the pan, put in a wire rack to Cool about 5 minutes. Slice

# Triple Chocolate Bread

**PREP: 10 MINUTES PLUS FERMENTING TIME /MAKES 1 LOAF**

## Ingredients

- 8 slices bread (1 pound)
- ⅔ cup milk, at 80°F to 90°F
- 1 egg, at room temperature
- 1½ tablespoons melted butter, cooled
- 1 teaspoon pure vanilla extract
- 2 tablespoons light brown sugar
- 1 tablespoon unsweetened cocoa powder

- ½ teaspoon salt
- 2 cups white bread flour
- 1 teaspoon bread machine or instant yeast
- ¼ cup semisweet chocolate chips
- ¼ cup white chocolate chips

**Directions**

**1. Preparing the Ingredients.**

Place the ingredients, except the chocolate chips, in your bread machine as recommended by the manufacturer.

**2. Select the Bake cycle**

Program the machine for Basic/White bread, select light or medium crust, and press Start.

When the machine signals, add the chocolate chips, or put them in the nut/raisin hopper and the machine will add them automatically.

When the loaf is done, remove the bucket from the machine.

Let the loaf cool for 5 minutes.

Gently shake the bucket to remove the loaf, and turn it out onto a rack to cool.

# Crusty Mustard Focaccia

**PREP: 10 MINUTES PLUS FERMENTING TIME /MAKES 8 SLICES**

**Ingredients**

- 2/3 cup water
- 1 tablespoon olive or vegetable oil
- 2 tablespoons spicy mustard
- 2¼ cups bread flour
- 1 tablespoon sugar
- 1 teaspoon table salt
- 1½ teaspoons bread machine or fast-acting dry yeast
- 3 tablespoons olive or vegetable oil
- Coarse (kosher or sea) salt, if desired

**Directions**

**1. Preparing the Ingredients.**

Measure carefully, placing all ingredients except 3 tablespoons oil and the coarse salt in bread machine pan in the order recommended by the manufacturer.

Select Dough/Manual cycle. Do not use delay cycle.

Remove dough from pan, using lightly floured hands. Knead 5 minutes on lightly floured surface (if necessary, knead in enough additional flour to make dough easy to handle). Cover and let rest 10 minutes.

**2. Select the Bake cycle**

Grease large cookie sheet. Roll or pat dough into 12-inch round on cookie sheet. Cover and let rise in warm place 10 minutes or until almost double.

Heat oven to 400°F. Prick dough with fork at 1-inch intervals or make deep depressions in dough with fingertips. Brush with 3 tablespoons oil. Sprinkle with coarse salt. Bake 15 to 18 minutes or until golden brown. Serve warm or cool.

# Sweet Vanilla Bread

**PREP: 10 MINUTES PLUS FERMENTING TIME /MAKES 1 LOAF**

## Ingredients

- 12 slice bread (1½ pounds)
- ½ cup + 1 tablespoon lukewarm milk
- 3 tablespoons unsalted butter, melted
- 3 tablespoons sugar
- 1 egg, at room temperature
- 1½ teaspoons pure vanilla extract
- ⅓ teaspoon almond extract
- 2½ cups white bread flour
- 1½ teaspoons bread machine yeast

## Directions

**1.    Preparing the Ingredients.**

Choose the size of loaf you would like to make and measure your ingredients.

Add the ingredients to the bread pan in the order listed above.

Place the pan in the bread machine and close the lid.

**2.   Select the Bake cycle**

Turn on the bread maker. Select the White/Basic setting, then the loaf size, and finally the crust color. Start the cycle.

When the cycle is finished and the bread is baked, carefully remove the pan from the machine. Use a potholder as the handle will be very hot. Let rest for a few minutes.

Remove the bread from the pan and allow to cool on a wire rack for at least 10 minutes before slicing.

# Chocolate Oatmeal Banana Bread

**PREP: 10 MINUTES PLUS FERMENTING TIME /MAKES 1 LOAF**

## Ingredients

- 12 to 16 slice bread (1½ to 2 pounds)
- 3 bananas, mashed
- 2 eggs, at room temperature
- ¾ cup packed light brown sugar
- ½ cup (1 stick) butter, at room temperature
- ½ cup sour cream, at room temperature
- ¼ cup sugar
- 1½ teaspoons pure vanilla extract
- 1 cup all-purpose flour
- ½ cup quick oats
- 2 tablespoons unsweetened cocoa powder
- 1 teaspoon baking soda

## Directions

**1.  Preparing the Ingredients.**

Place the banana, eggs, brown sugar, butter, sour cream, sugar, and vanilla in your bread machine.

Program the machine for Quick/Rapid bread and press Start.

While the wet ingredients are mixing, stir together the flour, oats, cocoa powder, and baking soda in a small bowl.

**2. Select the Bake cycle**

After the first fast mixing is done and the machine signals, add the dry ingredients.

When the loaf is done, remove the bucket from the machine.

Let the loaf cool for 5 minutes.

Gently shake the bucket to remove the loaf, and turn it out onto a rack to cool.

# SPECIALTY BREAD

## Best-Ever Oatmeal-Flax Bread

### PREP: 10 MINUTES /MAKES 1 LOAF

**Ingredients**
- 16 slice bread (2 pound)
- 1¼ cups lukewarm water
- 2 tablespoons vegetable oil or olive oil
- ¼ cup honey or maple syrup
- 1½ teaspoons table salt
- 3½ cups whole wheat flour
- ¼ cup sesame, sunflower, or flax seeds (optional)
- 1½ teaspoons bread machine yeast

**Directions**

**1. Preparing the Ingredients.**

Choose the size of loaf of your preference and then measure the ingredients.

Add all of the ingredients mentioned previously in the list.

Close the lid after placing the pan in the bread machine.

**2. Select the Bake cycle**

Turn on the bread machine. Select Whole Wheat/Wholegrain setting, select the loaf size, and the crust color. Press start.

When the cycle is finished, carefully remove the pan from the bread maker and let it rest.

Remove the bread from the pan, put in a wire rack to Cool about 5 minutes. Slice

## Bread Machine

### PREP: 10 MINUTES /MAKES 1 LOAF

**Ingredients**
- 1 cup all-purpose flour
- 2/3 cup packed dark brown sugar
- ½ cup old-fashioned oats
- 1/3 cup ground flaxseed or flaxseed meal
- 1 teaspoon baking soda
- 1 teaspoon salt
- 12/3 cups buttermilk

- 1 tablespoon old-fashioned oats

**Directions**

**1. Preparing the Ingredients.**

Choose the size of loaf of your preference and then measure the ingredients.

Add all of the ingredients mentioned previously in the list.

Close the lid after placing the pan in the bread machine.

**2. Select the Bake cycle**

Turn on the bread machine. Select White/Basic setting, select the loaf size, and the crust color. Press start.

When the cycle is finished, carefully remove the pan from the bread maker and let it rest.

Remove the bread from the pan, put in a wire rack to Cool about 5 minutes. Slice

# Panettone

**PREP: 10 MINUTES /MAKES 1 LOAF**

**Ingredients**

- ¾ cup warm water
- 6 Tbsp vegetable oil
- 1½ tsp salt
- 4 Tbsp sugar
- 2 eggs
- 3 cups bread flour
- 1 (¼ ounce) package Fleishman's yeast
- ½ cup candied fruit
- ⅓ cup chopped almonds
- ½ tsp almond extract

**Directions**

**1. Preparing the Ingredients.**

Add each ingredient to the bread machine in the order and at the temperature recommended by your bread machine manufacturer.

**2. Select the Bake cycle**

Close the lid, select the sweet loaf, low crust setting on your bread machine, and press start.

When the bread machine has finished baking, remove the bread and put it on a cooling rack.

# Christmas Bread

**PREP: 10 MINUTES /MAKES 8 SLICES**

**Ingredients**

- 1¼ cups warm whole milk (70°F to 80°F)
- ½ tsp lemon juice
- 2 Tbsp butter, softened
- 2 Tbsp sugar
- 1½ tsp salt
- 3 cups bread flour
- 2 tsp active dry yeast
- ¾ cup golden raisins

- ¾ cup raisins
- ½ cup dried currants
- 1½ tsp grated lemon zest
- Glaze:
- ½ cup powdered sugar
- 1½ tsp 2% milk
- 1 tsp melted butter
- ¼ tsp vanilla extract

**Directions**

**1. Preparing the Ingredients**

Add each ingredient except the raisins, currants, and lemon zest to the bread machine in the order and at the temperature recommended by your bread machine manufacturer.

**2. Select the Bake cycle**

Close the lid, select the sweet loaf, low crust setting on your bread machine, and press start.

Just before the final kneading, add the raisins, currants and lemon zest.

When the bread machine has finished baking, remove the bread and put it on a cooling rack.

Combine the glaze ingredients in a bowl.

Drizzle over the cooled bread.

# Challah Bread

**PREP: 10 MINUTES /MAKES 1 LOAF**

**Ingredients**

- 16 slice bread (2 pound)
- 1 cup +¾ teaspoon water, lukewarm between 80 and 90ºF
- 2 ½ tablespoons unsalted butter, melted
- 2 small eggs, beaten
- 2 ½ tablespoons sugar
- 1 ¾ teaspoons salt
- 4 ½ cups white bread flour
- 2 teaspoons bread machine yeast or rapid rise yeast

**Directions**

**1. Preparing the Ingredients.**

Choose the size of loaf of your preference and then measure the ingredients.

Add all of the ingredients mentioned previously in the list.

Close the lid after placing the pan in the bread machine.

**2. Select the Bake cycle**

Turn on the bread machine. Select Whole Wheat/Wholegrain setting, select the loaf size, and the crust color. Press start.

When the cycle is finished, carefully remove the pan from the bread maker and let it rest.

Remove the bread from the pan, put in a wire rack to Cool about 5 minutes. Slice

# Golden Brown

**PREP: 10 MINUTES /MAKES 1 LOAF**

**Ingredients**

- 12 slice bread (1½ pounds)
- ¾ cup +1 tablespoon water, lukewarm between 80 and 90ºF
- 2 tablespoons unsalted butter, melted
- 1 egg, beaten
- 2 tablespoons sugar
- 1 ½ teaspoons salt
- 3 ¼ cups white bread flour
- 1 ½ teaspoons bread machine yeast or rapid rise yeast
- For oven baking
- 1 egg yolk
- 2 tablespoons cold water
- 1 tablespoon poppy seed (optional)

**Directions**

**1.  Preparing the Ingredients.**

Choose the size of loaf of your preference and then measure the ingredients.

Add all of the ingredients mentioned previously in the list.

Close the lid after placing the pan in the bread machine.

**2.  Select the Bake cycle**

Turn on the bread maker. Select the Dough setting, then the loaf size, and finally the crust color. Start the cycle.

Lightly flour a working surface and prepare a large baking sheet by greasing it with cooking spray or vegetable oil or line with parchment paper or a silicone mat. Preheat the oven to 375°F and place the oven rack in the middle position.

After the dough cycle is done, carefully remove the dough from the pan and place it on the working surface. Divide dough in three even parts. Roll each part into 13-inch-long cables for the 1 ½ pound Challah bread or 17-inch for the 2-pound loaf. Arrange the dough cables side by side and start braiding from its middle part.

In order to make a seal, pinch ends and tuck the ends under the braid.

Arrange the loaf onto the baking sheet; cover the sheet with a clean kitchen towel. Let rise for 45-60 minutes or more until it doubles in size. In a mixing bowl, mix the egg yolk and cold water to make an egg wash. Gently brush the egg wash over the loaf. Sprinkle top with the poppy seed, if desired.

Bake for about 25-30 minutes or until loaf turns golden brown and is fully cooked.

# Mexican Sweet Bread

**PREP: 5 MINUTES /MAKES 12**

**Ingredients**

- 1 cup whole milk
- 1/4 cup butter
- 1 egg
- 1/4 cup sugar
- 1 teaspoon salt
- 3 cups bread flour
- 1 1/2 teaspoons yeast

**Directions**

1.  **Preparing the Ingredients.**

Add wet ingredients to bread maker pan.

Add dry ingredients, except yeast.

Make a well in the center of the dry ingredients and add the yeast.

2.  **Select the Bake cycle**

Set to Sweet Bread cycle, light crust color, and press Start.

Remove to a cooling rack for 15 minutes before serving.

# Irish Yogurt Bread

**PREP: 10 MINUTES /MAKES 8 WEDGES**

## Ingredients

- 1¾ cups all-purpose flour
- ½ cup dried currants or raisins
- 1½ teaspoons baking powder
- ¼ teaspoon baking soda
- ¼ teaspoon salt
- 1 container (6 oz) lemon burst, orange crème
- French vanilla yogurt 2 tablespoons vegetable oil

## Directions

1.  **Preparing the Ingredients.**

Choose the size of loaf of your preference and then measure the ingredients.

Add all of the ingredients mentioned previously in the list.

Close the lid after placing the pan in the bread machine.

2.  **Select the Bake cycle**

Turn on the bread machine. Select Whole Basic/White setting, select the loaf size, and the crust color. Press start.

When the cycle is finished, carefully remove the pan from the bread maker and let it rest.

Remove the bread from the pan, put in a wire rack to Cool about 10 minutes. Slice

# Dry Fruit Cinnamon Bread

**PREP: 10 MINUTES /MAKES 1 LOAF**

## Ingredients

- 12 slice bread (1½ pounds)
- 1¼ cups lukewarm milk
- ¼ cup unsalted butter, melted
- ½ teaspoon pure vanilla extract
- ¼ teaspoon pure almond extract
- 3 tablespoons light brown sugar
- 1 teaspoon table salt
- 2 teaspoons ground cinnamon
- 3 cups white bread flour
- 1 teaspoon bread machine yeast
- ½ cup dried mixed fruit
- ½ cup golden raisins, chopped

**Directions**

**1. Preparing the Ingredients.**

Choose the size of loaf of your preference and then measure the ingredients

Add all of the ingredients mentioned previously in the list except for the mixed fruit and raisins.

Close the lid after placing the pan in the bread machine.

**2. Select the Bake cycle**

Turn on the bread maker. Select the White/Basic or Fruit/Nut (if your machine has this setting) setting, then the loaf size, and finally the crust color. Start the cycle. When the machine signals to add ingredients, add the mixed fruit and raisins.

When the cycle is finished, carefully remove the pan from the bread maker and let it rest. Remove the bread from the pan, put in a wire rack to Cool about 10 minutes. Slice

# White Chocolate Cranberry Bread

**PREP: 10 MINUTES PLUS FERMENTING TIME /MAKES 1 LOAF**

**Ingredients**

- 12 slice bread (1½ pounds)
- ¾ cup plus 2 tablespoons milk, at 80°F to 90°F
- 1 egg, at room temperature
- 1½ tablespoons melted butter, cooled
- 1 teaspoon pure vanilla extract
- 2 tablespoons sugar
- ¾ teaspoon salt
- 3 cups white bread flour
- 1 teaspoon bread machine or instant yeast
- ½ cup white chocolate chips
- ⅓ cup sweetened dried cranberries

**Directions**

**1. Preparing the Ingredients.**

Place the ingredients, except the chocolate chips and cranberries, in your bread machine as recommended by the manufacturer.

**2. Select the Bake cycle**

Program the machine for Basic/White bread, select light or medium crust, and press Start.

When the loaf is done, remove the bucket from the machine.

Add the white chocolate chips and cranberries when the machine signals or 5 minutes before the last knead cycle ends.

Let the loaf cool for 5 minutes.

Gently shake the bucket to remove the loaf, and turn it out onto a rack to cool.

# Festive Raspberry Rolls

**PREP: 10 MINUTES PLUS FERMENTING TIME /MAKES 12 ROLLS**

**Ingredients**

- 1/3 cup milk
- 1/3 cup water
- 3 tablespoons butter, softened

- 1 egg
- 2 cups bread flour
- 1/3 cup sugar
- ½ teaspoon salt
- 1¾ teaspoons bread machine or fast-acting dry yeast
- 3 tablespoons raspberry preserves

**Directions**

**1.  Preparing the Ingredients.**

Measure carefully, placing all ingredients except preserves in bread machine pan in the order recommended by the manufacturer.

**2.  Select the Bake cycle**

Select Dough/Manual cycle. Do not use delay cycle.

Remove dough from pan, using lightly floured hands. Cover and let rest 10 minutes on lightly floured surface.

Grease 12 regular-size muffin cups. Roll or pat dough into 15×10-inch rectangle. Spread preserves over dough to within ¼ inch of edges. Starting with 15-inch side, roll up dough; pinch edge of dough into roll to seal. Stretch and shape roll to make even.

Cut roll into 12 equal slices. Place slices, cut side up, in muffin cups. Using kitchen scissors, snip through each slice twice, cutting into fourths. Gently spread dough pieces open. Cover and let rise in warm place about 25 minutes or until doubled in size. Dough is ready if indentation remains when touched. Heat oven to 375°F. Bake 15 to 20 minutes or until golden brown.

Immediately remove from pan to cooling rack. Serve warm or cool.

# Italian Easter Cake

**PREP: 10 MINUTES PLUS FERMENTING TIME /MAKES 4 SLICES**

**Ingredients**

- 1¾ cups wheat flour
- 2½ Tbsp quick-acting dry yeast
- 8 Tbsp sugar
- ½ tsp salt
- 3 chicken eggs
- ¾ cup milk
- 3 Tbsp butter
- 1 cup raisins

**Directions**

**1.  Preparing the Ingredients**

Add each ingredient except the raisins to the bread machine in the order and at the temperature recommended by your bread machine manufacturer.

**2.  Select the Bake cycle**

Close the lid, select the sweet loaf, low crust setting on your bread machine, and press start.

When the bread machine has finished baking, remove the bread and put it on a cooling rack.

# Beer Pizza Dough

**PREP: 10 MINUTES PLUS FERMENTING TIME /MAKES 1 LOAF**

**Ingredients**

- 12 slice bread (1½ pounds)
- 1 cup beer, at room temperature
- 3 tablespoons olive oil
- 1 tablespoon sugar
- 1 teaspoon table salt
- 3 cups white bread flour or all-purpose flour
- 1½ teaspoons bread machine yeast

**Directions**

**1. Preparing the Ingredients.**

Choose the size of loaf of your preference and then measure the ingredients

Add all of the ingredients mentioned previously in the list except for the mixed fruit and raisins.

Close the lid after placing the pan in the bread machine.

**2. Select the Bake cycle**

Turn on the bread maker. Select the Dough setting and then the dough size. Press Start

When the cycle is finished, carefully remove the dough from the pan.

Place the dough on a lightly floured surface and roll to make a pizza crust of your desired thickness. Set aside for 10–15 minutes. Top with your favorite pizza sauce, toppings, cheese, etc.

Bake in an oven at 400°F or 204°C for 15–20 minutes or until the edges turn lightly golden.

# Eggnog Bread

**PREP: 10 MINUTES PLUS FERMENTING TIME /MAKES 1 LOAF**

**Ingredients**

- 8 slice bread (1 pounds)
- ¾ cup eggnog, at 80°F to 90°F
- ¾ tablespoon melted butter, cooled
- 1 tablespoon sugar
- ⅔ teaspoon salt
- ¼ teaspoon ground cinnamon
- ¼ teaspoon ground nutmeg
- 2 cups white bread flour
- ¾ teaspoon bread machine or instant yeast

**Directions**

**1. Preparing the Ingredients.**

Choose the size of loaf of your preference and then measure the ingredients

Add all of the ingredients mentioned previously in the list except.

Close the lid after placing the pan in the bread machine.

**2. Select the Bake cycle**

Turn on the bread maker. Select the White/Basic setting, then the loaf size, and finally the crust color. Start the cycle.

When the cycle is finished, carefully remove the pan from the bread maker and let it rest. Remove the bread from the pan, put in a wire rack to Cool about 10 minutes. Slice

# Basil Pizza Dough

**Ingredients**

- 12 slice bread (1½ pounds)
- 1 cup lukewarm water
- 3 tablespoons olive oil
- 1 teaspoon table salt
- 1½ teaspoons sugar
- 1½ teaspoons basil, dried
- 3 cups white bread flour or all-purpose flour
- 1½ teaspoons bread machine yeast

**Directions**

**1.  Preparing the Ingredients.**

Choose the size of loaf of your preference and then measure the ingredients

Add all of the ingredients mentioned previously in the list.

Close the lid after placing the pan in the bread machine.

**2.  Select the Bake cycle**

Turn on the bread maker. Select the Dough setting and then the dough size. Press start.

When the cycle is finished, carefully remove the dough from the pan.

Place the dough on a floured surface and roll to make a pizza crust of your desired thickness. Set aside for 15 minutes. Top with your favorite pizza sauce, toppings and cheese.

Bake in an oven at 400°F or 204°C for 20 minutes or until the edges turn lightly golden.

# Whole-Wheat Challah

**PREP: 10 MINUTES PLUS FERMENTING TIME /MAKES 1 LOAF**

**Ingredients**

- 12 slice bread (1½ pounds)
- ¾ cup water, at 80°F to 90°F
- ⅓ cup melted butter, cooled
- 2 eggs, at room temperature
- 1½ teaspoons salt
- 3 tablespoons sugar
- 1 cup whole-wheat flour
- 2 cups white bread flour
- 1⅔ teaspoons bread machine or instant yeast

**Directions**

**1.  Preparing the Ingredients.**

Choose the size of loaf of your preference and then measure the ingredients.

Add all of the ingredients mentioned previously in the list.

Close the lid after placing the pan in the bread machine.

**2.  Select the Bake cycle**

Turn on the bread machine. Select Whole Wheat setting, select the loaf size, and the crust color. Press start.

When the cycle is finished, carefully remove the pan from the bread maker and let it rest.

Remove the bread from the pan, put in a wire rack to Cool about 10 minutes. Slice

# Classic Sourdough Bread

**PREP: 10 MINUTES PLUS FERMENTING TIME /MAKES 1 LOAF**

## Ingredients

- 12 slice bread (1½ pounds)
- 2 tablespoons lukewarm water
- 2 cups sourdough starter
- 2 tablespoons unsalted butter, melted
- 2 teaspoons sugar
- 1½ teaspoons salt
- 2½ cups white bread flour
- 1½ teaspoons bread machine yeast
- Sourdough Starter
- 2 cups lukewarm water
- 2 cups all-purpose flour
- 2½ teaspoons bread machine yeast

## Directions

**1. Preparing the Ingredients.**

Add the water, flour, and yeast to a medium-size non-metallic bowl. Mix well until no lumps are visible. Cover the bowl loosely and leave it in a warm area of your kitchen for 5–8 days. Do not place in a fridge or under direct sunlight.

Stir the mixture several times every day. Always put the cover back on the bowl afterward.

The starter is ready to use when it appears bubbly and has a sour smell.

Choose the size of loaf of your preference and then measure the ingredients. Add all of the ingredients mentioned previously in the list. Close the lid after placing the pan in the bread machine.

**2. Select the Bake cycle**

Turn on the bread machine. Select Whole Wheat setting, select the loaf size, and the crust color. Press start.

When the cycle is finished, carefully remove the pan from the bread maker and let it rest. Remove the bread from the pan, put in a wire rack to Cool about 10 minutes. Slice

# Portuguese Sweet Bread

**PREP: 10 MINUTES PLUS FERMENTING TIME /MAKES 1 LOAF**

## Ingredients

- 8 slice bread (1 pound)
- ⅔ cup milk, at 80°F to 90°F
- 1 egg, at room temperature
- 4 teaspoons butter, softened
- ⅓ cup sugar
- ⅔ teaspoon salt
- 2 cups white bread flour
- 1½ teaspoons bread machine or instant yeast

## Directions

**1. Preparing the Ingredients.**

Choose the size of loaf of your preference and then measure the ingredients.

Add all of the ingredients mentioned previously in the list.

Close the lid after placing the pan in the bread machine.

**2.  Select the Bake cycle**

Turn on the bread machine. Select Sweet setting, select the loaf size, and the crust color. Press start.
When the cycle is finished, carefully remove the pan from the bread maker and let it rest.

Remove the bread from the pan, put in a wire rack to Cool about 10 minutes. Slice

# Milk Honey Sourdough Bread

**PREP: 10 MINUTES PLUS FERMENTING TIME /MAKES 1 LOAF**

## Ingredients

- 16 slice bread (2 pounds)
- ½ cup lukewarm milk
- 2 cups sourdough starter
- ¼ cup olive oil
- 2 tablespoons honey
- 1⅓ teaspoons salt
- 4 cups white bread flour
- 1⅓ teaspoons bread machine yeast

## Directions

**1.  Preparing the Ingredients.**

Choose the size of loaf of your preference and then measure the ingredients.
Add all of the ingredients mentioned previously in the list.
Close the lid after placing the pan in the bread machine.

**2.  Select the Bake cycle**

Turn on the bread machine. Select White/ Basic setting, select the loaf size, and the crust color. Press start.
When the cycle is finished, carefully remove the pan from the bread maker and let it rest.

Remove the bread from the pan, put in a wire rack to Cool about 10 minutes. Slice

# Pecan Maple Bread

**PREP: 10 MINUTES PLUS FERMENTING TIME /MAKES 1 LOAF**

## Ingredients

- 16 slice bread (2 pounds)
- 1½ cups (3 sticks) butter, at room temperature
- 4 eggs, at room temperature
- ⅔ cup maple syrup
- ⅔ cup sugar
- 3 cups all-purpose flour
- 1 cup chopped pecans
- 2 teaspoons baking powder
- ½ teaspoon salt

## Directions

1.  **Preparing the Ingredients.**

Place the butter, eggs, maple syrup, and sugar in your bread machine.

2.  **Select the Bake cycle**

Program the machine for Quick/Rapid bread and press Start. While the wet ingredients are mixing, stir together the flour, pecans, baking powder, and salt in a small bowl. After the first fast mixing is done and the machine signals, add the dry ingredients. When the cycle is finished, carefully remove the pan from the bread maker and let it rest.

Remove the bread from the pan, put in a wire rack to Cool about 10 minutes. Slice

# Cherry Christmas Bread

**PREP: 10 MINUTES PLUS FERMENTING TIME /MAKES 1 LOAF**

## Ingredients

- 16 slice bread (2 pounds)
- 1 cup + 1 tablespoon lukewarm milk
- 1 egg, at room temperature
- 2 tablespoons unsalted butter, melted
- 3 tablespoons light brown sugar
- ⅛ teaspoon ground cinnamon
- 4 cups white bread flour, divided
- 1½ teaspoons bread machine yeast
- ⅔ cup candied cherries
- ½ cup chopped almonds
- ½ cup raisins, chopped

## Directions

1.  **Preparing the Ingredients.**

Choose the size of loaf you would like to make and measure your ingredients.

Add all of the ingredients except for the cherries, raisins, and almonds to the bread pan in the order listed above.

Close the lid after placing the pan in the bread machine.

2.  **Select the Bake cycle**

Turn on the bread machine. Select the White/Basic or Fruit/Nut (if your machine has this setting) setting, then the loaf size, and finally the crust color. Press start

When the machine signals to add ingredients, add the cherries, raisins, and almonds.

When the cycle is finished, carefully remove the pan from the bread maker and let it rest. Remove the bread from the pan, put in a wire rack to Cool about 10 minutes. Slice

# Nana's Gingerbread

**PREP: 10 MINUTE S PLUS FERMENTING TIME /MAKES 1 LOAF**

## Ingredients

- 8 slice bread (1 pound)
- ⅔ cup buttermilk, at 80°F to 90°F
- 1 egg, at room temperature
- 2⅔ tablespoons dark molasses
- 2 teaspoons melted butter, cooled
- 2 tablespoons sugar

- 1 teaspoon salt
- 1 teaspoon ground ginger
- ⅔ teaspoon ground cinnamon
- ⅓ teaspoon ground nutmeg
- ⅛ teaspoon ground cloves
- 2⅓ cups white bread flour
- 1⅓ teaspoons bread machine or active dry yeast

**Directions**

**1. Preparing the Ingredients.**

Place the ingredients in your bread machine as recommended by the manufacturer.

**2. Select the Bake cycle**

Program the machine for Sweet bread and press Start. When the cycle is finished, carefully remove the pan from the bread maker and let it rest. Remove the bread from the pan, put in a wire rack to Cool about 10 minutes. Slice

# Coffee Caraway Seed Bread

**PREP: 10 MINUTE S PLUS FERMENTING TIME /MAKES 1 LOAF**

**Ingredients**
- 12 slice bread (1½ pounds)
- ¾ cup lukewarm water
- ⅓ cup brewed coffee, lukewarm
- 1½ tablespoons balsamic vinegar
- 1½ tablespoons olive oil
- 1½ tablespoons dark molasses
- ¾ tablespoon light brown sugar
- ¾ teaspoon table salt
- 1½ teaspoons caraway seeds
- 3 tablespoons unsweetened cocoa powder
- ¾ cup dark rye flour
- 1¾ cups white bread flour
- 1½ teaspoons bread machine yeast

**Directions**

**1. Preparing the Ingredients.**

Choose the size of loaf of your preference and then measure the ingredients.

Add all of the ingredients mentioned previously in the list.

Close the lid after placing the pan in the bread machine.

**2. Select the Bake cycle**

Turn on the bread machine. Select Whole wheat/ Wholegrain setting, select the loaf size, and the crust color. Press start.

When the cycle is finished, carefully remove the pan from the bread maker and let it rest.

Remove the bread from the pan, put in a wire rack to Cool about 10 minutes. Slice

# Bread Machine Brioche

## Ingredients

- 12 slice bread (1½ pounds)
- ½ cup plus 1 tablespoon milk, at 80°F to 90°F
- 3 eggs, at room temperature
- 2 tablespoons sugar
- ¾ teaspoon salt
- 3 cups white bread flour
- 1½ teaspoons bread machine or instant yeast
- ½ cup (1 stick) butter, softened

## Directions

### 1. Preparing the Ingredients.

Choose the size of loaf of your preference and then measure the ingredients.

Add all of the ingredients mentioned previously in the list.

Close the lid after placing the pan in the bread machine.

### 2. Select the Bake cycle

Turn on the bread machine. Select White/ Basic setting, select the loaf size, and the crust color. Press start.

When the cycle is finished, carefully remove the pan from the bread maker and let it rest.

Remove the bread from the pan, put in a wire rack to Cool about 10 minutes. Slice

# Sun-Dried Tomato Rolls

**PREP: 10 MINUTE S PLUS FERMENTING TIME /MAKES 12 ROLLS**

## Ingredients

- ¾ cup warm milk (105°F to 115°F)
- 2 cups bread flour
- ¼ cup chopped sun-dried tomatoes in oil, drained, 1 tablespoon oil  reserved 1 tablespoon sugar
- 1 teaspoon salt
- 1½ teaspoons bread machine yeast

## Directions

### 1. Preparing the Ingredients.

Measure carefully, placing all ingredients in bread machine pan in the order recommended by the manufacturer.

### 2. Select the Bake cycle

Select Dough/Manual cycle. Do not use delay cycle.

Remove dough from pan; place on lightly floured surface. Cover and let rest 10 minutes Lightly grease cookie sheet with shortening or spray with cooking spray.

Gently push fist into dough to deflate. Divide dough into 12 equal pieces. Shape each piece into a ball. Place balls about 2 inches apart on cookie sheet. Cover and let rise in warm place 30 to 45 minutes or until almost doubled in size.

Heat oven to 350°F. Bake 12 to 16 minutes or until golden brown. Remove from cookie sheet to cooling rack. Serve warm or cool.

# Cinnamon Beer Bread



**Ingredients**

- 16 slice bread (2 pounds)
- 2 cups beer, at room temperature
- 1 cup unsalted butter, melted
- ⅓ cup honey
- 4 cups all-purpose flour
- 1⅓ teaspoons table salt
- ⅓ teaspoon ground cinnamon
- 1⅓ tablespoons baking powder

**Directions**

**1. Preparing the Ingredients.**

Choose the size of loaf of your preference and then measure the ingredients.

Add all of the ingredients mentioned previously in the list.

Close the lid after placing the pan in the bread machine.

**2. Select the Bake cycle**

Turn on the bread machine. Select Quick/ Rapid setting, select the loaf size, and the crust color. Press start.

When the cycle is finished, carefully remove the pan from the bread maker and let it rest.

Remove the bread from the pan, put in a wire rack to Cool about 10 minutes. Slice

# Traditional Paska

PREP: 10 MINUTE S PLUS FERMENTING TIME /MAKES 1 LOAF

**Ingredients**

- 12 slice bread (1½ pounds)
- ¾ cup milk, at 80°F to 90°F
- 2 eggs, at room temperature
- 2 tablespoons butter, melted and cooled
- ¼ cup sugar
- 1 teaspoon salt
- 2 teaspoons lemon zest
- 3 cups white bread flour
- 2 teaspoons bread machine or instant yeast

**Directions**

**1. Preparing the Ingredients.**

Choose the size of loaf of your preference and then measure the ingredients.

Add all of the ingredients mentioned previously in the list.

Close the lid after placing the pan in the bread machine.

**2. Select the Bake cycle**

Turn on the bread machine. Select Basic/ White setting, select the loaf size, and the crust color. Press start.

When the cycle is finished, carefully remove the pan from the bread maker and let it rest.

Remove the bread from the pan, put in a wire rack to Cool about 10 minutes. Slice

# French Butter Bread


**PREP: 10 MINUTES PLUS FERMENTING TIME /MAKES 1 LOAF**

## Ingredients
- 12 slice bread (1½ pounds)
- ½ cup + 1 tablespoon lukewarm milk
- 3 eggs, at room temperature
- 2 tablespoons sugar
- ¾ teaspoon table salt
- ½ cup unsalted butter, melted
- 3 cups white bread flour
- 1½ teaspoons bread machine yeast

## Directions
**1. Preparing the Ingredients.**

Choose the size of loaf of your preference and then measure the ingredients.

Add all of the ingredients mentioned previously in the list.

Close the lid after placing the pan in the bread machine.

**2. Select the Bake cycle**

Program the machine for Basic / White bread and press Start.

About 10 minutes before the end of your first kneading cycle, begin adding the butter, 1 tablespoon each minute.

When the cycle is finished, carefully remove the pan from the bread maker and let it rest.

Remove the bread from the pan, put in a wire rack to Cool about 10 minutes.